THE CATHOLIC UNIVERSITY OF AMERICA
CANON LAW STUDIES
No. 124

THE EUCHARISTIC FAST

AN HISTORICAL SYNOPSIS AND COMMENTARY

A DISSERTATION

Submitted to the Faculty of Canon Law of the Catholic University of America in Partial Fulfillment of the Requirements for the Degree of

DOCTOR OF CANON LAW

BY THE

REV. THOMAS FRANCIS ANGLIN, J.C.L.
Missionary of Our Lady of LaSalette

THE CATHOLIC UNIVERSITY OF AMERICA PRESS
WASHINGTON, D.C.

1941

Imprimi Potest:

PAULUS M. REGAN, M.S.,
Superior Provincialis.
Hartfordiae, Conn., die 2 iunii 1941.

Nihil Obstat:

CLEMENTIUS V. BASTNAGEL, J.U.D.,
Censor Deputatus.
Washingtonii, D.C., die 3 iunii 1941.

Imprimatur:

✠ MICHAEL J. CURLEY, D.D.,
Archiepiscopus Baltimorensis.
Baltimorae, Md., die 4 iunii 1941.

PRINTED IN THE UNITED STATES OF AMERICA
BY THE PUBLICATION PRESS, BALTIMORE, MD.

TO MY MOTHER

TABLE OF CONTENTS

PART TWO

CANONICAL COMMENTARY

PREFACE

The object of all observances prescribed by the Church in the administration and reception of the Blessed Eucharist is to show due reverence to the Adorable Sacrament, and to bring out by symbolic ceremonies the truths of the Mystery. For a worthy reception of the Holy Eucharist, not only are certain dispositions of soul required but a preparation of the body is also demanded by the Church. The disposition of the body most strictly enjoined is that the communicant be fasting. This precept, which obliges under pain of mortal sin, is called the natural or Eucharistic fast. It consists in abstaining from all food and drink, and even from anything which is taken as medicine, from midnight to the time of reception of Holy Communion.

The present dissertation has for its purpose an attempt to treat in detail the historical, canonical, moral, and casuistical aspects of the law of the Eucharistic fast. The great antiquity of the practice of fasting before Mass and the reception of Holy Communion has been readily taken for granted, but of the growth of the actual legislation of the Eucharistic fast, comparatively very little has been commonly known. Nothing can be of greater assistance in supplying a better understanding of present ecclesiastical discipline than to study the history of a question and to see by what norms the Church's legislation in the past has been determined on the subject. Any question concerning the Sacraments is necessarily of a canonico-moral nature, and there is difficulty in looking at it merely under the aspect of ecclesiastical law. However, in the historical synopsis an attempt will be made to consider the subject solely with reference to the question: What doctrine respecting the Eucharistic fast is set forth in ecclesiastical legislation? Necessarily, in the commentary a great number of moral theologians have had to be consulted, since the canonists have left the treatment of this question to the moral theologians, because of the many moral issues which are involved in the canonical interpretation of the law of the natural fast. However, throughout the dissertation an effort has been made to distinguish between the explanation of the law of the Eucharistic fast according to the principles of moral theology, and the interpretation of the law in accordance with the principles of ecclesiastical jurisprudence.

The writer wishes to take this occasion to express his gratitude, first of all, to the Very Reverend Paul M. Regan, M.S., Provincial Superior of the American Province of the Missionaries of Our Lady of LaSalette for the opportunity afforded him of pursuing the study of Canon Law at the Catholic University of America; to the Faculty of the School of Canon Law for their ready and generous assistance at all times; and his sincere thanks to all who aided in the preparation of this dissertation.

PART ONE
HISTORICAL SYNOPSIS

INTRODUCTION

The purpose of the law of the Eucharistic fast can be easily understood. This precept was introduced into the canons of the Church to insure all the reverence possible for the great Sacrament of the Body and Blood of Christ, and to prevent abuses. The reasons for the prohibition of food and drink before Communion are stated as follows by Saint Thomas: "First, . . . that it (the Blessed Sacrament) may enter into a mouth not yet contaminated by any food or drink; secondly, because of its signification, *i.e.,* to give us to understand that Christ, Who is the reality of this Sacrament, and His Charity, ought to be first of all established in our hearts . . . thirdly, on account of the danger of vomiting and intemperance, which sometimes arises from overindulgence in food. . ."[1]

One thing is certain, that there is no divine precept as regards receiving Holy Communion fasting. This is clear from the fact that Christ and the Apostles were not fasting at the institution of the Holy Eucharist, nor is there any evidence that such a divine positive precept was given after the Last Supper. It is merely an ecclesiastical law, yet founded on the natural law of reverence for holy things, among which the Eucharist is by far the first and foremost.

Nor certainly is there any divine precept commanding the faithful to receive the Sacred Body and Blood after having partaken of food and drink.[2] The words of Christ

[1]*Summa Theologica* (6 vols., Taurini: Marietti, 1932), Pars III q. LXXX, a. 8; Translation taken from Pohle-Preuss, *The Sacraments* (4 vols., St. Louis 1917), II, 270.

[2] Cyprianus, *Epistola LXIII*—Migne, *Patrologiae Cursus Completus, Series Latina* (221 vols., Parisiis: 1864), IV, 386-387.

at the Last Supper, "Do this in commemoration of Me," were not a command on the part of Christ to receive Holy Communion after a common meal, such as He had partaken of with His disciples on Holy Thursday in the Upper Room; but they were an order to continue this Sacrifice and Sacrament in the Church for all ages, in perpetual praise and adoration of God, and for the spiritual food of the faithful.

The obligation of the Eucharistic fast is an ecclesiastical law, from which the Holy See can, and at times does, dispense. Nor is the law absolute. It admits of exceptions in certain cases, for example, when the Holy Eucharist is administered as Viaticum, or when there is necessity of preventing the profanation of the Blessed Sacrament.[3] The Rubrics of the Roman Missal likewise state exceptional cases in which a priest is allowed to say Mass after having broken his fast.[4] Likewise an exception is made in favor of the sick, under certain circumstances and conditions, whereby they are allowed to receive Holy Communion although they are not able to keep the natural fast in its entirety.[5] Besides these canonical exceptions, authors give as reasons for additional exceptions such cases, as the avoidance of public scandal, or the procuring of Viaticum by the celebration of Mass, in an extraordinary circumstance, where the Holy Eucharist could not otherwise be had.[6]

[3] Canon 858, ¶ 1.

[4] *Missale Romanum, ex Decreto Sacrosancti Concilii Tridentini Restitutum S. Pii V Postificis Maximi, jussu editum, aliorum Pontificum cura Recognitum a Pio X Reformatum et SSmi. D. N. Benedicti XV, auctoritate vulgatum.* (Ratisbone: Sumptibus ex Typis Friderica Pustet, 1925), tit. *De defectibus in celebratione missarum occurrentibus*, c. III, *de defectu panis*, n. 5; c. IV *de defectu vini*, n. 5; IX, *de defectibus dispostionis corporis.*

[5] Canon 858, ¶ 2.

[6] Cappello, *Tractatus Canonico-Moralis de Sacramentis*, Vol. I, *De Sacramentis in Genere, de Baptismo, Confirmatione et Eucharistia*, 3 ed., Romae: Marietti, 1938; Vermeersch-Creusen, *Epitome Iuris Canonici*, 3 vols. (Vol. I, 6 ed., Vols. II and III, 5 ed.), Romae: Dessain, 934–1937, II, 45; Augustine, *A Commentary on Canon Law*, (8 vols., St. Louis: Herder, 1918-1922) IV, 234.

CHAPTER I

THE EUCHARISTIC FAST IN THE FIRST FOUR CENTURIES

ARTICLE 1. THE AGAPE AND THE EUCHARISTIC FAST

Although our Blessed Saviour instituted the Sacrament of the Most Holy Eucharist after He had first eaten of the Jewish Passover Supper with His disciples, nevertheless, the Church, taught by His divine magisterium, decrees that this Sacred Mystery should not be celebrated except by priests who are fasting: nor received by the faithful unless they likewise are fasting.

There are many reasons why Christ should have chosen such an occasion for the institution of the Eucharist. The Judaic ritual prescribed that on the evening of the fourteenth day of Nisan, all families should gather together their members and partake of the Paschal supper to commemorate the sparing of the Hebrews in Egypt when God smote the firstborn of the Egyptians. Christ, being a faithful observer of the Mosaic Law, wished to fulfill the legal ceremonies of the Jewish Rite. As the Venerable Bede remarked, the Apostles were not fasting because it was necessary that they observe the legal Pasch before partaking of the true Pasch of the New Dispensation.[7] Moreover, it was because of the symbolism of the Paschal Lamb as applied to Himself that Christ took this occasion to institute the new Sacrament of His Body and Blood, thereby putting an end to the ancient sacrifice of the Old Law. It was most reasonable that Christ should have celebrated this Pasch

[7] *In Lucae Evangelium Expositio*, Lib. VI—MPL, XCII, 595.

with His disciples for the last time, and that as a token of His love should have at its close instituted this Sacrament, which is the new Pasch.

It is not certain whether it was the custom for the first Christians, following the example of Christ, to celebrate the Sacred Mysteries after a supper, taken in common. Historians and liturgical writers are not agreed as to just what was the practice followed in the time of the Apostles, with regard to the Eucharistic liturgy. The complete absence of formal ecclesiastical legislation in the writings witnessing Tradition in the first centuries, render it impossible to pronounce with certainty on the origin of the Eucharistic fast. That it is a very early Church discipline is, however, commonly admitted by all. Some authors even attribute its institution to the time of the Apostles. But in truth, of the very beginnings of this practice but little is definitely known. However, it is certain beyond all doubt, that the law ordering all to come to the Holy Eucharist fasting may be traced to very ancient custom or rule, if not to the legislative action of the Apostles themselves.

Vasquez,[8] Bona,[9] and Suarez[10] are of the opinion that the fast was of Apostolic institution, and was always observed in the Church. They explain that the *Agape,* or common repast among the early Christians took place, not before, but after the Sacred Mysteries. This latter is the exegesis of Chrysostom,[11] Jerome, [12] and Theodoret[13] in the first Epistle to the Corinthians.

[8] *Libri Commentariorum ac Disputationum in Tertiam Partem S. Thomae* (2 vols., Lugduni: 1631), disp. CCXI, art. 8, cap. 1.

[9] *Rerum Liturgicarum Libri Duo* (Coloniae: 1674), lib. I, cap. 21.

[10] *Opera Omnia* (ed. nova, 30 vols., Parisiis: 1866), *De Sacramento Eucharistiae,* disp. LXVIII, sect. 3.

[11] *Homilia XXXVII in Epistolam I ad Corinthios*—Migne, *Patrologiae Cursus Completus, Series Graeca* (161 vols., Parisiis: 1864), LXI, 227-235.

[12] *Commentarium in Epistolam I ad Corinthios—MPL,* XXX, 751.

[13] *Interpretatio Epistolae I ad Corinthios,* cap. XI—*MPG,* LXXXII, 314.

However, no positive historical proof for the opinion that the fast was always observed in the Church can be brought forth, and the opinion is commonly rejected by modern authors as being without foundation.[14]

The more common teaching concerning the Eucharist has been substantially as follows: that the first Christians in imitation of the *quasi-sacred* ritual of the Paschal Supper continued the practice of a common repast, usually known as the *Agape,* and intimately associated with the Blessed Eucharist, so intimately in fact, as to form the preparatory rite which led up to the Sacrament and Sacrifice.[15] This custom was observed at least in the churches of Jerusalem and Corinth, and was presumably of almost universal observance.[16] This habit of taking food and drink in the assembly led to serious abuses, and consequently, as early as the time of St. Paul's first Epistle to the Corinthians, it was necessary to reform the custom. At the beginning of the second century the *Agape* ceased to serve its primary purpose—that of a preparation for the Eucharist—but it continued as an observance of *quasi-liturgical* character, taking place in the Church, being conducted by the clergy, and accompanied by prayers and blessings.[17]

[14] Many, *Praelectiones de Missa cum Appendice de Sanctissimo Sacramento Eucharistiae* (Parisiis: 1903), p. 321; Funk, "L'Agape," *Revue d'Histoire Ecclésiastique de Louvain,* IV (1903), 5-22; Funk, *Manual of Church History* (2 vols., translated from the fifth German edition by Luigi Cappadelta, St. Louis: 1910), I, 65; Fortescue, *The Mass, A Study of the Roman Liturgy* (New York: Kenedy, 1929), p. 86; Cabrol, *Origines Liturgiques* (Paris: 1906), p. 135; Chardon, *Histoire des Sacréments* (4 vols., Paris: 1885), II, *De l'Eucharistie,* 199; Corblet, *Histoire du Sacrément de l'Eucharistie* (2 vols., Paris: 1895), I, 318.

[15] Cf. *supra,* preceding footnote.

[16] Husslein, *The Mass of the Apostles* (New York: Kenedy, 1929), Acts, II, 42; Acts, II, 46; I Cor., 21; p. 94; La Bauche, *The Three Sacraments of Initiation, Baptism, Confirmation, and Holy Eucharist* (New York: Benziger, 1922), p. 399; cf. the authors mentioned in footnote 14.

[17] Tertullian, *Apologia XXXIX—MPL,* II, 470; Canons of Hippolytus, c. 35—Roberts-Donovan, *Anti-Nicene Fathers* (10 vols., Translations of the Fathers down to A. D. 325, New York: Scribners, 1903), V, 256; Council of Gangra (There is some difficulty in determining the exact date of this Council. Mansi places it about 324. Harduin puts

This common teaching of a Eucharistic *Agape* was attacked by Battifol in his *Etudes d'Histoire et de Théologie Positive.* He denied not only the liturgical character of the *Agape,* and its connection with the Holy Eucharist in the early Church, but even its very existence as a primitive institution.[18] Funk, in 1903, took up the question, and wrote in defense of the traditional opinion that the Eucharistic service was preceded by a meal taken in common.[19] In the same year Gillis wrote a lengthy account of the Christian *Agape* in the Catholic University Bulletin, giving an exhaustive exposition of the controversy, likewise upholding the existence of a primitive *Agape,* before the reception of Holy Communion.[20] Ladeuze entered into the discussion with an article published by the Revue Biblique under the title of *"Pas d'Agape dans la Première Epître aux Corinthiens,"* in which he gave partial support to the stand taken by Monsignor Battifol that there was no evidence of a Eucharistic *Agape* in the eleventh chapter of the I Epistle to the Corinthians.[21]

However, it must be remarked that the question of an *Agape* did not concern itself with the Eucharistic fast as such. It is evident that if the *Agape* existed, and did precede the Eucharistic service there can be no question of a fast. But a denial of the *Agape* would not necessarily postulate the necessity of a Eucharistic fast. Nor would the existence of a primitive liturgical *Agape* necessarily exclude all possi-

it at 330. It is placed between 324-358.), c. 11—Mansi, *Sacrorum Conciliorum Nova et Amplissima Collectio* (58 vols., Parish Leipzig-Arnhem; 1901), II, 1102; Council of Laodicea (343-381), c. 18—Mansi, II, 569.

[18] *Etudes d'Histoire et de Théologie Positive* (première série, quatrième édition, Paris: Librairie Victor Lecoffre, 1906), pp. 283 and 329; Cf. also, "Agape," *Dictionnaire de Théologie Catholique* (14 vols., Paris: 1903-1939), I, 551.

[19] "L'Agape," *Revue d'Histoire Ecclésiastique de Louvain,* IV (1903), 5-22; "Tertullien et l'Agape," *op. cit.,* V (1904), 5-15.

[20] "The Christian Agape," *Catholic University Bulletin,* IX (1903), 465-508.

[21] "Pas d'Agape dans la Première Epître aux Corinthiens," *Revue Biblique (nouvelle série),* I (1904), 78-81.

bility of the fast, if the *Agape* did not precede the Eucharist, but was held subsequent to it.

A brief review of the texts of Sacred Scripture in which there is reference to the Eucharistic service will be necessary for a better understanding of the question. In the *Acts of the Apostles,* II, 42 and II, 46, we read of the "breaking of bread." Does the phrase "breaking of bread" have reference to the Eucharist alone, or does it include the Sacramental and non-Sacramental rite of an *Agape?* All are unanimous in their opinion that it certainly has reference at least to the Eucharist.[22]

However, Fortescue,[23] Husslein,[24] Keating,[25] Cabrol,[26] Gillis,[27] and Leclercq[28] cite this passage as undeniable proof also for the existence of an *Agape,* in connection with the Eucharist. This is the almost universal interpretation. "Saint Luke, it is true, mentions the *Agape* after the Breaking of the Bread, but it does not follow that Saint Luke here literally follows the historic order."[29] Battifol rejects entirely this interpretation that there is question of a Eucharistic *Agape* in these texts.[30]

So much for the extent of the practice followed in the primitive Church of Jerusalem. The life of the then recently converted Church of Corinth, is described by St. Paul in

22 Cf. *supra,* footnote 16.

23 "There were two functions of the first Christian assemblies which disappeared after the first century. These were the Love Feast, "*Agape*". . . . From the order of Acts II, 42 (the teaching of the Apostles, "Communion," breaking of bread, prayers), still more from the invariable order we find in later documents, we may conclude that the Eucharist came at the end of the other service."—*A Study of the Roman Liturgy,* p. 5.

24 *The Mass of the Apostles,* p. 86.

25 *The Agape and the Eucharist in the Early Church* (London: 1901), p. 69.

26 *Origines Liturgiques,* p. 135.

27 "The Christian Agape," *Catholic University Bulletin,* IX (1903), 474.

28 "Agape," *Dictionnaire d'Archéologie Chrétienne et de Liturgie* (14 vols., Paris: Librairie Letouzey et Ane, Boulevard Raspail, 87, 1924-), I (première partie), 785.

29 Husslein, *The Mass of the Apostles,* p. 86; cf. also Fortescue, *A Study of the Roman Liturgy,* p. 5.

30 *Etudes d'Histoire et de Théologie Positive,* p. 285.

his I Epistle to the Corinthians. The setting of the text in the discussion is as follows: St. Paul, who while on his third missionary journey, is brought news of disorders which have arisen in the Church of Corinth, writes to the Corinthians, and reproves them for their conduct. In the eleventh chapter he condemns the abuses of their assembly. It will be best to quote the entire text for a clearer understanding of the exegesis:

> When you come therefore together into one place, it is not now to eat the Lord's Supper. For everyone taketh before his own supper to eat. And one indeed is hungry and another is drunk. What, have you not houses to eat and to drink in? Or despise ye the Church of God; and put them to shame that have not? What shall I say to you? Do I praise you? In this I praise you not. For I have received of the Lord that which also I delivered unto you, that the Lord Jesus, the same night in which He was betrayed, took bread, and giving thanks, broke, and said: Take ye, and eat: this is My Body, which shall be delivered for you: this do for the commemoration of Me. In like manner also the chalice, after He had supped, saying: This chalice is the new testament in my blood: this do ye as often as you shall drink for the commemoration of Me. For as often as you shall eat this bread and drink the chalice, you shall show the death of the Lord until He come. Therefore whosoever shall eat this bread or drink the chalice of the Lord unworthily, shall be guilty of the body and of the blood of the Lord. But let a man prove himself; and so let him eat of that bread, and drink of the chalice. For he that eateth and drinketh unworthily, eateth and drinketh judgment to himself, not discerning the body of the Lord. . .Wherefore, my brethren, when you come together to eat, wait for one another. If any man be hungry, let him eat at home; that you come not together unto judgment. And the rest I will set in order, when I come.[31]

To what has Paul reference here? To the Eucharist alone, to the *Agape* only, or to an *Agape* joined to the celebration of the Eucharist? Was the *meal* of which Saint Paul speaks an authorized liturgical function, and did it take place before the Eucharistic service? What is the

[31] I Cor. XI, 20-29; 33-34.

attitude of Paul toward the abuses that he reproves? Attention is drawn to this text in particular for it is not only strongly in favor of the previous existence of a Eucharistic *Agape*, but it may also be the departure point in a change of discipline demanding a fast of some sort before the consecration and administration of the Eucharist.

To go into detail as regards the exegesis of various authorities on this text would not be practical. As a general rule they may be divided into two classes—those who hold that Paul speaks of the Eucharist only, and gives no sanction to a common meal or *Agape*, but to condemn it as an innovation; and the second class, the defenders of the primitive Eucharistic *Agape*, who see here a clear reference to an *Agape* held in connection with the Holy Eucharist, and serving as a preparatory rite to it. Paul, they assert, does not condemn the *Agape* but only the abuses that have associated themselves with it.

The principal defender of the first opinion is Battifol, who was the first to deny the traditional interpretation. St. Paul, Battifol tells us, forbids any eating besides the reception of the Holy Eucharist, and sternly rebukes the Corinthians who have introduced the partaking of profane food. It is not a question of abuses only; the very principle of combining a meal with the Sacrament is condemned. "The gross attempt made of such a union is emphatically reproved," says Battifol.[32] But it will be remembered that even Battifol does not postulate a Eucharistic fast. "Without doubt, Paul does not impose the law of fast, but he intends that the Eucharistic Supper should not be held in

32 "Ces réunions chrétiennes ne sont point faites pour rassasier. . . Mais telle n'est pas la pratique des Corinthiens. . . . St. Paul ne dit point aux Corinthiens: Quand vous vous réunirez désormais, puisque l'usage est de joindre à l'eucharistie un repas en commun, que ce repas soit vraiment commun et que chacun ait une part égale. L'apôtre ne dit rien de pareil. Il exprime, aussi nettement qu'on peut souhaiter, que se réunir pour autre chose que pour la coupe et le pain eucharistique, . . . c'est faire autre chose que le repas du Seigneur. Quiconque veut manger à sa faim et boire à sa soif n'a qu'à rester chez soi."—*Etudes d'Histoire et de Théologie Positive*, pp. 289-290; Cf. also "Agape", *Dictionnaire de Théologie Catholique*, I, 551.

connection with a bodily repast."[33]

Ladeuze[34] and Thomas[35] are of the same opinion. They infer that if Saint Paul has reference to a repast here, it is not to an authorized practice, but to a custom introduced by the Corinthians themselves, on their own initiative. Paul in writing to them, condemns not only the abuses that took place in the assembled meal, but the very institution itself, that is, the presuming to partake of a supper before the Eucharist. These authors make no mention of the law of Eucharistic fast.

Leclercq,[36] Funk,[37] Keating,[38] Gillis,[39] Labauche[40] and in general all who uphold the primitive *Agape* argue from this text, that at Corinth, as in Jerusalem, a common meal of some sort was the custom before the Eucharistic Communion. They are of the opinion that Paul did not condemn it, or abolish it, but merely corrected whatever abuses it had become subject to, for they argue the *Agape* continued on as related to the Eucharist for at least the remainder of the century, and longer.

Labauche says, "Our Savior instituted the Eucharist after he had first eaten the Jewish Pasch with His disciples. Hence, in the earliest times, it was the custom to celebrate the Eucharist after a meal taken in common. This practice was certainly followed in Jerusalem (Acts, II, 42), Corinth

33 "Agape," *Dictionnaire de Théologie Catholique,* I, 551.

34 "Pas d'Agape dans la Première Épître aux Corinthiens," *Revue Biblique* (nouvelle série), I (1904), 79-81.

35 "Agape," *Dictionnaire de la Bible* (5 vols., 3 suppléments, Paris-Vi: Librarie Letouzey et Ane, Boulevard Raspail, 87, 1895-1938), Suppl. I, 145-147.

36 "Agape," *Dictionnaire d'Archéologie Chrétienne et de Liturgie,* I (première partie), 785.

37 "L'Agape," *Revue d'Histoire Ecclésiastique de Louvain,* IV (1903), 5-22.

38 *The Agape and the Eucharist in the Early Church,* p. 69.

39 "The Christian Agape," *Catholic University Bulletin,* IX (1903), 474.

40 *The Three Sacraments of Initiation, Confirmation, and Holy Eucharist,* p. 401.

(I Cor. XI), and Smyrna (*Ignatius ad Symrn.* n. 8). It must have spread nearly everywhere."[41]

Saint Augustine, who tells us that the Eucharistic fast was observed universally in his time, attributes the institution of it to Saint Paul on his third voyage to Corinth. Augustine deduces his conclusions from these words, "And the rest I will set in order when I come."[42] Benedict XIV does not think the fact of Apostolic origin improbable. Treating of this question he says: *"Nec desunt qui eius originem repetunt ab aevo apostolico."*[43]

Authorities are inclined to grant little credence to this statement of Augustine, remarking that in matters of historic fact the Fathers of the Church have no more authority than other authors. Since, moreover, Augustine gives no proof for what he says, his assertion is not accepted by all. Keating, who sees in I Corinthians a common meal and a Eucharistic Communion, supposes that Saint Paul, on account of the disorders in the Corinthian assemblies, later separated the *Agape* from the Eucharist.[44] Corblet is of the opinion that Saint Paul tried to reform the practice of the *Agape,* but it continued, nevertheless, for some time, in certain churches, especially in Africa.[45] Prat also believes that Saint Paul did not abolish the *Agape,* but believes that the separation of the *Agape* from the Eucharist took place very early.[46]

Funk considers the fast correlative with the morning celebration of the Eucharist. He admits that at a very early date the celebration was transferred to the morning. According to him this change may have occurred towards

[41] Labauche, *loc. cit.*

[42] *Epistola ad Januarium, Epistola LIV—MPL,* XXXIII, 203.

[43] *De Synodo Dioecesana* (4 vols., Mechliniae: 1842), lib. VI, cap. 8, n. 10.

[44] *The Agape and the Eucharist in the Early Church,* p. 50.

[45] *Histoire du Sacrement de l'Eucharistie* (2 vols., Paris: 1885), I, 318.

[46] *La Théologie de St. Paul* (5 ed., Paris: 1908-1913). pp. 166-167.

the end of the Apostolic period, possibly as a reform of the abuses already prevalent in the time of Saint Paul in the evening service of the *Agape,* or it may have been a result of Trajan's decree the *hataeriae,* or illicit nocturnal gatherings.[47]

About the year 112, Pliny, at that time governor of Bythynia, wrote to his master, the Emperor Trajan, to ask how he was to treat the Christians. He described what he had learned of this sect from Christians who had apostasized under torture. "They affirmed, however, the whole of their guilt, or their error, was, that they were in the habit of meeting on a certain fixed day (*stato die*) before it was light (*ante lucem*), when they sang in alternate verses a hymn to Christ, as to a god, and bound themselves by a solemn oath not to do any wicked deeds (*seque sacramento non in scelus aliquod obstringere*), . . . after which it was their custom to separate, and then reassemble to partake of food—but food of an ordinary and innocent kind (*cibum promiscuum tamen et innoxium*). Even this practice, however, they had abandoned after the publication of my edict, by which according to your orders, I had forbidden political associations."[48]

The traditional opinion is that the second assembly was the *Agape.* From the Latin construction this latter was the one that was abandoned. It could not have been the Eucharistic assembly that was renounced. For it would be hard to understand how the Christians would have abandoned the Eucharist, which was the very center of their religious life.

Gillis says that in all probability these two assemblies were not connected. There were two meetings—the social gathering in the evening; its feature being the partaking of food in common. The other meeting was held in the morning; its feature, in the words of the governor, was "*sacra-*

[47] *Manual of Church History,* I, 165.

[48] Text and Translation taken from Melmoth, *Pliny Letters* (2 vols., Cambridge: Harvard University Press, 1935), 402-405.

mento se obstringere". It is not clear what the word '*sacramento*" means in this letter of Pliny. It may have already attained its technical meaning of "the mystery", and so may, in Pliny's letter, indicate the Holy Eucharist.[49]

Tertullian used the word "*sacramentum eucharisticum*", and speaks of it being celebrated "*in antelucanis coetibus*".[50] Ramsay is of the opinion that the Christians declared to have renounced, not the reunion *ante lucem*, but the later reunion. For he says that this repast in common constituted a sodality or *hataeriae*, which was prohibited by edict, whereas to assemble for the purpose of singing religious hymns was not forbidden.[51]

As Gillis remarks, if the sacrament was indeed the Eucharist, and the *cibum promiscuum*, on the other hand, was the *Agape*, the conclusion is of no little significance—that at least in one of the provinces, in the first years of the second century, the *Agape* had ceased to be connected with the Eucharist.[52] Funk says, "The practice of fasting before Communion is mentioned even by Tertullian, and doubtless it goes back to the time when the Eucharist began to be celebrated in the morning."[53] Schaff puts the date of separation of the *Agape* and the Eucharist at the beginning of the second century, placing the Communion in the morning, and the love feast in the evening. However, he does not mention the fast.[54] Chardon says there was no absolute rule on the subject of the Eucharistic fast, and it would be impossible to determine when the rule to receive Holy Communion fasting was made. He remarks, that it would have been very difficult for the first Christians to receive fasting, since

[49] "The Christian Agape," *Catholic University Bulletin*, IX (1903), 492-493.

[50] *De Corona Militis*, cap. III—*MPL*, II, 70.

[51] *The Church in the Roman Empire* (New York: 1893), p. 219 ff.

[52] "The Christian Agape," *Catholic University Bulletin*, IX (1903), 492.

[53] *Op. cit.*, I, 166.

[54] *History of the Christian Church* (7 vols., New York: 1894-1896), II, 239.

they assembled only in secret, and there was no fixed hour for the celebration of the Sacred Mysteries, but the people came together whenever they could.[55]

The conclusion of the defenders of a primitive Eucharistic *Agape,* are not opposed to the antiquity of the practice of fasting before Communion. Granting that the *Agape* did serve as a preparatory rite to the Eucharist, it is certain that the practice did not continue for long. The majority of authorities usually place the date in the first years of the second century. Due to lack of historical evidence in the first two centuries it is impossible to be more specific about the origin of the fast. Though left in the dark as to the actual facts, it is possible that when the *Agape* was disconnected from the Eucharist, and the Eucharistic celebration was transferred from the evening to the early morning hours, the Eucharistic fast was an almost automatic consequence. There is no indication whatsoever of a prescribed law to this effect, but it certainly did offer an occasion for the custom which is found existing at the end of the second century.

Article 2. First Evidences of Positive Legislation

Among the decrees of Pope Soter, who ruled the Church from 167-175, there is a formal prohibition for any priest to say Mass after having partaken of the slightest amount of food or drink, with the exception of completing the Holy Sacrifice in case a priest was taken sick during Mass. The penalty of excommunication was attached to the violation of this precept.[56]

That it was the custom in Africa to fast prior to receiving

[55] *Histoire des Sacrements* (4 vols., Paris: 1745), II, De l'Eucharistie et de la Pénitence, 199.

[56] Mansi, I, 691. This decree is not found in the MSS. of Harduin, *Acta Conciliorum et Epistolae Decretales ac Constitutiones Summorum Pontificum* (12 vols., Parisiis: 1715); XI Council of Toledo (675), c. 14—Mansi, XI, 145.

Communion is witnessed by Tertullian in the beginning of the third century. Writing to a Christian woman he speaks of the difficulty for a Christian wife to conceal from her pagan husband *what she eats in secret before all other food.*[57] That the food to which he refers, which was taken in secret, was the bread of the Eucharist appears from the fact that in another epistle he relates the ancient custom in the Church of giving the Blessed Eucharist to the faithful to carry home with them to be consumed in private. He also speaks of certain scrupulous persons who resigned themselves only with difficulty to go to Communion on fast days, as if by that the fast was broken. He advises them to take the Body of the Lord home with them from the sacrificial altar and consume it after the period of fasting is over.[58]

The obligation of the Eucharistic fast is also denoted in the Canons of Hippolytus (217-235), who has left us a codification of the ritualistic discipline of his time.[59] Leclercq places the date of the *Canons of Hippolytus* as early as 195, and says that the best critics see in this document a synodal account of the Roman Church dating from that time.[60]

Likewise in the Oriental Church, in the beginning of the fourth century, there are found evidences of the Eucharistic fast having the force of law. "No one may partake in the Sacrifice," says Saint Basil, "if he is not fasting."[61] The work of Timothy of Alexandria, second successor of

57 *Ad uxorem* (lib. II, cap. V): "Non sciet maritus, quid secreto ante omnem cibum gustes; et si sciverit omnem, non illum credit esse qui dicitur?"—*MPL*, I, 1296.

58 *De Oratione*, c. 14—*MPL*, I, 1181-1183.

59 *Canons of Hippolytus* (n. 205): "Ne gustet aliquis fidelium quidquam nisi antea de mysteriis sumpserit, praesertim diebus ieiunii sacri."—Tixeront, *Précis de Patrologie* 4è éd., Paris: Victor Lecoffre, 1920), p. 283; *Anti-Nicene Fathers*, p. 256, n. 28; Duchesne, *Origines due Culte Chrétien* (troisième édition, Paris: 1902), Appendix, p. 517.

60 ¶ *Dictionnaire d'Archéologie Chrétienne et de Liturgie*, I, 805.

61 "Neque enim fieri potest, ut absque ieiunio audeat sacerdos ad sacrum ministerium accedere, non tantum in mystico horum temporum vero cultu, verum etiam in eo qui iuxta legem mosaicam in figuris peragebatur."—*De Ieiunio, Homilia* I, n. 6—*MPG*, XXXI, 171.

Saint Athanasius, whose canonical work was later incorporated into the Oriental ecclesiastical law, denotes a rigorous observance of the Eucharistic fast.[62] Saint Gregory Nazienzen has these words: "Christ delivered the Mystery of the Pasch in the Supper Room, and at a supper the day before His Passion, we, however, in the Church, and before supper (i. e. fasting), after the Resurrection."[63]

Elsewhere at the same time the law of sacramental fast was in force. Saint John Chrysostom advises the faithful to fast that they may be worthy to communicate.[64] Indirectly he establishes the same principle when he admonishes those who are not fasting to come to church with the others, not to communicate, but to listen to the sermon.[65] And in *Epistle CXXV*, writing from exile to the Patriarch Cyriac, against his calumniators, he says: "My enemies have charged that I had given communion to some persons who were not fasting. But if I did this, let my name be erased from the list of bishops, that it may not be inscribed in the book of the Orthodox Church, that Jesus Christ may exclude me from His kingdom."[66] These words of justification written to the patriarch, tell us of the horror that the Christians of the fifth century manifested when confronted with the violation of the law of the Eucharistic fast.

[62] "Si quis ieiunans ut communicet, os lavans, vel in balneo aquam bibit nolens, debetne communicare? Sane, ubi etiam invenit Satanas occasionem prohibendi eum a communione, frequentius hoc faciet." Pitra, *Iuris Ecclesiastici Graecorum Historia et Monumenta, Iussu Pii IX, Pont. Max. Curante* (2 vols., Vol. I, a Primo P. C. N. ad VI Saeculum, Romae: 1864), I, 634.

[63] *Oratio XL*: "Ille Christus paschatis mysterium discipulis in coenaculis tradidit, et a coena, et unico ante passionem die; nos in templis, et ante coenam (i. e., ieiuni), et post Resurrectionem."—*MPG*, XXXVI, 402; cf. Bona, *Rerum Liturgicarum*, lib. I, cap. 21.

[64] *Homilia XXVII*, in I Corinthios: "Tu vero antequam percipias quidem, ieiunias, ut quomodocumque videaris."—*MPG*, LXI, 23.

[65] *Homilia IX ad Populum Antiochenum*—*MPG*, XLIX, 103.

[66] "Multa adversum me strexerunt: aiuntque me post epulas quibusdam communionem impertisse. Hoc si feci, de episcoporum libro nomen meum expungatur, nec in orthodoxae fidei volumine scribatur, quoniam ecce si quidquam eiusmodi perpetravi, Christus e regno suo me abjiciat."—*MPG*, LII, 683.

Saint Augustine testifies to the universality of the practice of fasting before Communion in his day. He says, that so it has pleased the Holy Spirit, that in honor of so great a Sacrament, the Body of the Lord should pass into the mouth of a Christian before all other food.[67]

[67] *Epistola ad Januarium, Epistola LIV*: "Num quid tamen propterea calumiandum est universae Ecclesiae, quod a ieiunis semper accipitur? Ex hoc enim placuit Spiritui Sancto, ut in honorem tanti Sacramenti, in os Christiani prius dominicum corpus intraret, quam ceteri cibi: nam ideo per universum orbem mos iste servatur."—*MPG*, XXXIII, 203.

Chapter II

FROM THE FOURTH CENTURY TO THE DECREE OF GRATIAN (1139)

Article I

Legislation Relative to the Celebration of Mass

While it was the universal discipline in the infant Church that no one receive Communion if not fasting, yet there are evidences that for centuries this discipline was not observed everywhere and at all times without exception. These exceptions were either abuses or they were particular customs restricted to local Churches, and seemingly tolerated, such as the evening service in the Church of Africa on the anniversary day of the Lord's Supper. Some abuses crept in unnoticed through a gradual relaxation of fervor; others were introduced contrary to the law by certain heretical sects, such as the Priscillianists in Spain, who taught that a fast was not necessary before partaking of the Sacred Mysteries. There are not wanting numerous decrees of various councils, both local and general, which show that the Church was always vigilant to condemn these errors and abuses.

The Council of Hippo in 393 decreed, "That the Sacraments of the Altar are to be received fasting."[68] This decree was confirmed by the III Council of Carthage in 397. "We have ordained," says the Council, "that the Sacraments of the Altar are not to be celebrated by any but those who are

[68] Mansi, III, 896.

fasting, except on the anniversary day on which the Lord's Supper is celebrated."[69]

The origin of celebrating the Sacred Mysteries on Holy Thursday after an *Agape* is unknown. It may have been a survival of the primitive Eucharistic *Agape*. Saint Augustine testifies to this custom, and it was recognized as lawful by him, since he did not condemn it. It was meant to reproduce the Last Supper in detail, *"tamquam ad insigniorem commemorationem,"* says the Bishop of Hippo.[70] This practice lasted in the Church for many centuries, but was forbidden in the Council of Constantinople (The Trullan Synod) in 692, lest the Lenten fast be broken.[71] Strabo, in the ninth century, witnesses that the fast was observed even on Holy Thursday.[72]

The III Council of Carthage (397) condemned another custom which was beginning to take root in the African Church. When a person died, burial took place on the same day, and since it was the practice not to bury the faithful unless Mass was said for them with the body present, some priests were wont to perform the obsequies and to say Mass in the afternoon or evening, while not fasting. This abuse was forbidden, and henceforth for an afternoon funeral service, whether it was for a bishop, a cleric, or one of the faithful, only prayers were ordinarily to be said. The celebration of Mass was not to be tolerated, if the priest who

[69] C. 29—Mansi, III, 885.

[70] *Epistola ad Januarium*—*MPL*, XXXIII, 204.

[71] Council of Constantinople, c. 29: "Carthaginensis synodi canon dicit, ut sancta altaris non nisi a sobriis hominibus peragantur, excepto uno die in anno, in quo coena domini peragitur; tunc fortasse propter aliquas in iis locis occasiones ecclesiae utiles sanctis illis patribus hac dispensatione usis. Cum nihil ergo nos inducat, ut accuratam observationem relinquamus, statuimus apostolicas ac paternas traditiones sequentes, non oportere in quadragesimae postrema septimana quinta feria ieiunium solvere, et totam quadragesimam iniuria afficere."—Mansi XI, 955.

[72] *De rebus Ecclesiasticis*: "Si itaque illo die coenae dominicae post prandium communicare non licet, cui et exemplum Domini et quorumdam assensus suffragii videbatur, multo minus aliis temporibus licet, . . ."—*MPL*, CXIV, 940.

conducted the service had already broken his fast.[73]

Moreover, in the forty-eighth chapter of this same Council it is said that this custom (of fasting) was confirmed in the Nicene Council (325). It is worthy of note that the canon uses the word *confirmatum* and not *institutum.*[74] However, in the decrees of the Council of Nice that are extant, no reference can be found to this confirmation spoken of in the Council of Carthage. The exact number of disciplinary canons drawn up in the Council of Nice has been a matter of dispute, but the number twenty is not universally accepted in all recognized collections.[75]

Socrates, narrating events which took place towards the end of the fourth century, testifies to the universal practice of fasting, and at the same time relates a custom contrary to the general rule. He says that the Egyptians in the vicinity of Alexandria and the Thebaid did not follow the example of other Christians, who celebrated the Sacred Mysteries fasting, but that after they had eaten, and were filled with all manner of foods, Mass was said in the evening and Communion distributed.[76]

Sozomen, a contemporary of Socrates narrates the same.[77]

[73] *III Carthage,* cap. 29: Ut sacramenta altaris nonnisi a ieiunis hominibus celebrentur, excepto uno die anniversario quo coena domini celebratur. Nam si/ aliquorum, pomeridiano tempore defunctorum, sive episcoporum, seu clericorum, sive ceterorum, commendatio facienda est, solis orationibus fiat, si illi qui faciunt, iam pransi inveniantur."—Mansi, III, 885; cf. Thurston, "My Sacrifice and Yours," *ER,* XCI (1934), 565-557.

[74] *III Carthage,* cap. 48: "De fide enim Nicaeni tractatus audivimus. Verum et de sacrificiis inhibendis post prandium, ut a ieiunis, sicut dignum est, offerantur, et tunc et nunc confirmatum est."—Mansi, III, 891.

[75] Schroeder, *Disciplinary Decrees of the General Councils* (St. Louis Mo.: B. Herder Book Co., 1937), p. 17.

[76] *Historia Ecclesiae,* lib. V: "Non tamen, sicut mos est Christianorum sacra mysteria percipiunt. Postquam enim epulati sunt, et omni genere ciborum saturati, sub vesperam oblationen facta communicant."—*MPG,* LXVII, 635.

[77] *Historia Ecclesiae,* lib. VII: "In multis autem urbibus ac vicis Aegypti, contra receptam omnium consuetudinem, die Sabbati sub vesperam convenientes, iam pransi, sacramenta percipiunt."—*MPG,* LXVII, 1478.

Evidently these were abuses, as both Socrates and Sozomen remark: "They do not, however, receive the Sacred Mysteries (fasting), as is the custom of other Christians," and "against the universally accepted custom." Nor was it the universal practice even in these parts. Bishop Pallodius (died about 431), writing the life of the Abbot Appullo in the Thebaid, witnessed that the monks were wont to go to Communion fasting.[78]

The II Council of Braga (563) revoked the ancient custom of an evening Mass on Holy Thursday. The decree of the Council does not appear to be concerned expressly with the African custom maintained in Hippo and Carthage, but seems rather to be directed against an error of that time, which seems to have had its origin from Priscillian, for Priscillian revived the false teachings already reproved in the III Council of Carthage, namely, that priests who were not fasting should be allowed to celebrate Mass for the dead in the afternoon. The Council of Braga anathematized this error, and extended the condemnation even to the non-fasting celebration of Thursday in Holy Week.[79]

Nine years later the III Council of Braga (572) again condemned the error and ruled that any priest who was found violating the precept of the Eucharistic fast was to be deprived of his office, and deposed by his bishop.[80]

The wording of the canon may be noted, *quocumque iam cibo percepto.* This is the first indication there is of the stringency with which the Eucharistic fast binds, so that it

[78] *Historia Lausiaca,* c. 52: "Qui enim cum ipso erant fratres, alimentum non prius accipiebant, quam Eucharistiae Christi Communicassent: hoc autem faciebant, hora nona diei."—*MPG,* XXXIV, 1149.

[79] C. 16—Mansi, IX, 776; cf. Bona, *Rerum Liturgicarum,* lib. I, cap. 21, n. 2.

[80] C. 10: "Si quis presbyter post hoc edictum nostrum amplius in hac vesania fuerit reprehensus ut nec ieiunus, sed quocumque iam cibo percepto, oblationem consecraverit, continuo ab officio suo privatus, a proprio deponatur episcopo."—Mansi, IX, 841; cf. VII Council of Toledo, c. 2—Mansi, X, 767-768.

is broken by even the smallest possible quantity of food that is consumed. While no mention is made here of the same rigor exercised against one taking anything in liquid form, there is no reason for thinking that it would not equally apply in that case, especially since less than a hundred years later the VII Council of Toledo (646) explicitly includes liquids as well as solid foods.[81]

The majority of the Oriental writers likewise showed themselves most rigorous in the matter of the Eucharistic fast. The testimonies of Saint Basil,[82] Saint Gregory Nazienzen,[83] and Saint John Chrysostom,[84] are proof of this. Then too, in an Armenian Synod, celebrated at Dovin in Armenia, in 527, a decree is found which prescribes: "No one must partake of anything before Communion; and if the minister knows that anyone has already done so, he must not communicate him."[85]

The Syrians, as well as the Greeks, maintained the principle of the Eucharistic fast, though in practice they admitted exceptions condemned in the Western Church. For instance, according to their canons, one would not be hindered from going to Communion, if by mistake he took anything liquid before dawn; especially if this happened on a major feast, and because of the solemnity the person

[81] C. 2: "Ne tamen quod naturae languoris causa consulitur, in praesumptionis perniciem convertatur, nullus post cibi potuve (cibum potumve) quamlibet (quemlibet) minimum sumptum missas facere, nullus absque patenti proventu molestiae, minister vel sacerdos, cum coeperit, imperfecta officia praesumat omnino relinquere. Si quis haec tentare praesumpserit, excommunicationis sententiam sustinebit."—Mansi, X, 767-768.

[82] *De Ieiunio, Homilia* I, n. 6—*MPG*, XXXI, 171

[83] *Oratio XL*—*MPG*, XXXVI, 402.

[84] *Homilia XXVII in I ad Corinthios*—*MPG*, 231; *Epistola CXXV ad Cyriacum*—*MPG*, LII, 683.

[85] Hefele, *History of the Church Councils* (translated from the German, edited by William Clark, vols., 2 ed., Edinburg: 1883-1896). IV 147; cf. Pitra, (*Ius Ecclesiasticum Graecorum*, I, 103): "Si quis aqua ore hausta communicat, in exercratione sit."

wanted to receive Holy Communion.[86] Moreover, there was some disagreement among them as to the time when the fast began. Some canons declared the fast obliged from sunset of the previous evening, while others imposed it only from midnight on.[87]

In Rome, the practice of fasting before Mass prevailed so strictly that when the Roman Pontiff was to celebrate two Masses on the same day, it was prescribed that after the first Mass he was not to wash out his mouth. This is testified to in the Gregorian Sacramentary, edited by Hugo Menard, a Benedictine monk, at the beginning of the seventh century.[88]

The same law of fast was also imposed on the deacon and

86 *Resolutiones Canonicae Jacobi Edesseni*: "Nemini licet cibum aliquem aut potum quemcumque capere ante sacramentorum sumptionem, nisi urgente morbi necessitate, aut in mortis periculo. Et si quis ex errore biberit potum simplicem in aliquo festo ac petierit communionem donari, sacerdotis iussu communicet, accepto prius canone."—Lamy, *Dissertatio de Syrorum Fide et Disciplina in Re Eucharistica*, p. 183. Reference to this work henceforth will be made as follows: Lamy, *De Syrorum Fide et Disciplina. Resolutiones Canonicae Ioannis Telae*: "Si ante diluculum homo aquam biberit, ieiunus tamen sit, existimo quod possit accedere et accipere consecrata, modo conscientia eius non sit dubia." Lamy *De Syrorum Fide et Disciplina*, p. 71. These two works date from the sixth and seventh centuries. cf. Lamy, *De Syrorum Fide et Disciplina*, pp. 173 and 214; cf. Many, *Praelectiones de Missa cum Appendice de Sanctissimo Sacramento Eucharistiae*, p. 321.

87 *Quaestiones et Responsa Michaelis Melichae*, n. 21: "Qui nocte siti fatigatus bibit, licetne ei ut mane sequenti communionem accipiat?" R. "Si id ante mediam noctem contigerit, licet; si deinde, non licet."

In another place the canons of the same Bishop state: "Si matutino tempore communio celebrabitur, cavebit unusquisque ne post occasum solis, edat aut bibat: quando vero edit aut bibit, non licet ei eodem die Eucharistiam accipere."—Lamy, *De Syrorum Fide et Disciplina*, p. 183; cf. Corblet, *Hist. du Sacr. de l'Euch.*, I, 332.

88 "Quando Apostolicus duas Missas celebrat una die inter eas non lavat os, nisi post officium; sed absque intervallo, finita priore, incipitur altera."—*MPL*, LXXVIII, 123; cf. *MPL*, LXXVIII, 395, where in a note Menard, gives as the reason for this rubric danger lest some drops of water should be swallowed, thus preventing one from going to Holy Communion; cf. Many, *Praelectiones de Missa cum Appendice de Sanctissimo Sacramento Eucharistiae*, p. 324.

subdeacon of the altar by the Council of Auxerre in 578.[89] The reason for this canon is, that it was not permitted at that time for anyone to serve at the altar or to be present at the Holy Sacrifice, unless he communicated at the same time with the celebrant.[90] There was also the precept, binding not only clerics, but all the faithful, to assist at High Mass fasting, as will be seen later on in the history of the Eucharistic fast.[91]

That France was not immune from the abuses of some priests who dared to say Mass after having broken their fast, and even in some cases while in a state of inebriation, is clear from the II Council of Macon (585). The reason given by this Council for its law is that it is an insult to set corporal food above the spiritual food of the Eucharist. Likewise, a penalty was inflicted on delinquent priests; "the loss of any dignity or honor."[92]

While the Council cites the ancient canon of Carthage and makes mention of the practice of evening Mass in the African Church, yet it did not intend to approve the custom in France of celebrating Mass in the evening, but only to confirm the canon decreed by Carthage, excluding however, the exception of Holy Thursday. This is clear from the ruling of the Council which is absolute.[93]

The Council held at Constantinople, commonly known as the Trullan Synod, abrogated the African custom of celebrating Mass in the evening on Holy Thursday; saying that the Holy Fathers may have at that time, because of some

[89] C. 19: "Non licet Presbytero, aut Diacono, aut Subdiacono post acceptum cibum vel poculum Missas tractare, aut in Ecclesia, dum Missae dicuntur stare."—Mansi, IX, 914.

[90] Cf. Bona, *Rerum Liturgicarum,* lib. I, cap. 21. n. 2.

[91] Cf. *infra,* p.

[92] C. 6: "Item decernimus, ut nullus presbyter, confertus cibo, aut crapulatus vino, sacrificia contrectare. . .praesumat."—Mansi, IX, 952; Hefele-Leclercq, *Histoire des Conciles* (10 vols., Paris: 1909), III, 209-210.

[93] II Council of Macon, c. 6: "Nullus presbyter . . . sacrificia contrectare praesumat."—Mansi, IX, 952.

particular occasion useful to the Church in Africa, made use of that dispensation, but that the reasons were no longer valid, and that henceforth all were to follow the Apostolic and Patristic tradition, i. e., of the Eucharistic fast.[94]

The Council of Laodicaea (343-381) had made the same rule for the fast on Holy Thursday. However, the canon of the Council of Laodicaea had precise reference to the ecclesiastical fast of Holy Thursday and omitted any explicit mention of the Eucharistic fast, and to the evening Mass of Holy Thursday.[95]

Archbishop Hincmar, (+882), in a *capitulum* ordered the priests in the diocese of Rheims to remain fasting up to a late hour of the day so that they could succor the necessities of the dead, and also the necessities of the sick and of pilgrims.[96] This canon was later incorporated into the *Decree of Gratian,* which was published in the middle of the twelfth century (1139).[97] This *Decree* also incorporated the ancient canon of the III Council of Carthage ordering the priest to be fasting for the celebration of the Holy Sacrifice of the Mass.[97a]

Robert Sala, a Cistercian, in his *Adnotationes ad Bona* relates that the abuse of non-fasting priests celebrating afternoon funeral Masses continued in the monasteries of his community till the thirteenth century, so that if one of the monks died in the afternoon, it was the custom to have

[94] Synod of Trullo (692), c. 29—Mansi, XI, 955; this Council was meant to furnish disciplinary decrees which were wanting in the V (553) and VI (680-681) General Councils of Constantinople.

[95] C.50—Mansi, II, 572.

[96] *Capitula Hincmarensis,* c. 9—Mansi, XV, 477.

[97] C. 2, D. XCI: "Deinde peractis horis, infirmis visitatis, si voluerit ad opus rurale exeat ieiunus, ut iterum necessitatibus peregrinorum et hospitum sive diversorum commeantium, infirmorum quoque ac defunctorum succurere possit usque ad statutam horam pro qualitate temporis et opportunitate."

[97a] C. 49, D. I, *de cons.*

Mass said for him, even though the priest had taken the ablutions in his Mass earlier in the day.[98]

Abbot Regino in the tenth century, in a booklet on ecclesiastical discipline, advises the bishop, on the occasion of his canonical visit, to question the pastor if he celebrated Mass around the third hour, and after that, remained fasting till midday, in order to say Mass for travellers if necessary.[99]

In this contingency there evidently was an implicit permission to binate. The Capitulum of Hincmar implied a like permission.[100]

A peculiar ruling is noted in the eleventh century. While in the enactments of the Councils in the Western Church no time was specified for the beginning of the fast, since it appears that the Fathers of the Councils understood a fast from midnight, which was the beginning of the Roman day; yet in the Council of Selingstad, it was forbidden for a priest who had taken anything after cockcrow in summer to say Mass on the same day. The Council ruled the same for winter time, except in cases of necessity.[101]

This ruling is rather unique. However, Gregory of Tours also made use of the expression "*galli cantus*" in reference to the Eucharistic fast. He related that a priest named Epachus, who was known to have taken something to drink after cockcrow, did not fear to mount the altar, and that at the moment of Communion, he was taken with a fit of epilepsy, and obliged to reject the Sacred Species.[102]

[98] Cf. Many, *Praelectiones de Missa cum Appendice de Sanctissimo Sacramento Eucharistiae*, p. 329.

[99] Benedictus XIV, *De Synodo Dioecesana*, lib. VI, cap. 8, n. 2; *MPL*, CXXXII, 188.

[100] C. 9—Mansi, XV, 447.

[101] C. 4: "Decretum est etiam in eodem concilio, ut presbyter aliquis post galli cantum aestibus noctibus bibens, proximo die missam non celebrat: hiemalibus similiter, nisi necessitas cogat."—Mansi, XIX, 397; Landon, *A Manual of the Councils of the Holy Catholic Church* (London: 1846), p. 226.

[102] *De Gloria Martyrum*—*MPL*, LXXI, 782.

ARTICLE 2

THE EUCHARISTIC FAST AND THE COMMUNION OF INFANTS

The II Council of Macon (585),[103] after having recalled the general discipline of the Church regarding the Eucharistic fast, made the following peculiar ruling: that on Wednesday and Friday, whatever particles remained in the *sacrarium* were to be dipped in wine, and then distributed to the little children, *innocentes*, who were to be fasting. The reference here is to the particles which were kept in the *sacrarium* for the sick, and the Council for some reason of its own wished them to be given to the children.[104] It is evident from this canon that the fast was imposed even on little children.

According to the usage which prevailed in the early ages of the Church, the Eucharist was also administered to infants immediately after baptism. The reason for this practice may have been the erroneous belief that the Holy Eucharist was necessary for eternal salvation. Corblet, however, denies this, and prefers the opinion that the practice of infant Communion was introduced, not because it was considered necessary for salvation, but to provide an added help against diabolical obsessions.[105] It was declared in the Council of Trent that the Holy Eucharist was not necessary for salvation for children who had not attained the use of reason. However, the Council did not condemn the ancient practice of giving Communion to these children, and remarked that it was not to be condemned, since the Fathers of the Church must have had some reason for their

103 C. 6: "Quaecumque reliquiae sacrificiorum post peractam missam in sacrario supersederint, quarta vel sexta feria innocentes ab illo cujus interest, ad ecclesiam adducantur, et indicto eis ieiunio, easdem reliquias conspersas vino percipiant."—Mansi, IX, 952.

104 Vasquez, *In Summa D. Thomae*, Disp. CCXI, quaest. 80, n. 2; cap. 5.

105 *Hist. du Sacr. de l'Euch.*, I, 306.

manner of acting.[106] This custom of infant Communion had already ceased in the Western Church in the twelfth century.[107]

Saint Cyprian[108] and Saint Augustine[109] speak of this practice of administering Communion to infants. Pope Innocent I (402-417)[110] and Pope Gelasius I (482-496)[111] in their writings seem to have indicated a permanent relation between Baptism and Communion, since apparently they considered both Baptism and Communion necessary for eternal salvation. However, their writings should be considered in the light of the fact that according to the discipline of their day, Communion was always administered immediately after Baptism.

A Roman Ordo of the sixth or seventh century taught that no food, not even from the breast, should be given to the little children who were to receive Communion. The fast was imposed for one hour, i. e., from the time of their Baptism till the reception of the Holy Eucharist.[112] The same ruling is repeated in the Ancient Rite of the Church of Poitiers in the ninth century.[113]Another Roman Ordo, however, did not make this ruling absolute, but allowed for

[106] Sess. XXI, *de communione sub utraque specie et parvulorum*, can. 4; cf. Canon 854, ¶1.

[107] Benedictus XIV, ep. "*Quadam*," 24 mart. 1756, ¶7—*Fontes*, n. 439.

[108] De Lapsis—*MPL*, IV, 484.

[109] *Epistola ad Bonifacium*—*MPL*, XXXIII, 361; *Epistola ad Vitalem Pelagianum*—*MPL*, XXXIII, 984.

[110] *Epistola ad Patres Concilii Milevantani*—*MPL*, XXXIII, 785.

[111] *Epistola VII ad mones episcopos per Picenum*—*MPL*, XIX, 37-38.

[112] *Ordo Romanus I*—*MPL*, LXXVIII, 957-958; *Ordo Romanus VII*—*MPL*, LXXVIII, 1000; Cf. Benedictus XIV, *De Synodo Dioecesana*, lib. VI, cap. 8, n. 4.

[113] "Illud vero observandum est, ut postquam baptizati fuerint infantes, nullum cibum accipiant, nec ablactentur antequam communicant, et per septem dies paschae ad missas procedant et offertur pro eis et communicant."—Martène, *De Antiquis Ritibus Ecclesiae* (ed. novissima, 3 vols., Rotomagi: 1700-1702), I, 430; cf. p. 427 (as to the Church of Treves); p. 440 (as to the Church of Apames in Syria); p. 44 (as to the Church of Besançon); cf. also Leclercq, *Dictionnaire d'Archéologie*, III, 2443.

cases of necessity.[114] The practice of administering Communion to infants continued for a long time in the Greek Church and even in the eighteenth century it was still the custom in many Oriental Churches, though in some Churches of the Oriental Rite it was forbidden. In the time of Benedict XIII (1724-1730), the question was asked of the Sacred Congregation of the Propagation of Faith by the Melchites: "Whether Communion was to be administered to infants immediately after Baptism?" The answer was given: "Children are not bound to receive Communion but where the ancient custom is in vogue, it is not to be condemned."[115]

In a Council held at Monte Libano or Mount Lebanon in Italy in 1736 for the Italo-Greeks it was decreed that notwithstanding the prescriptions of the ancient ritual concerning the administration of the Eucharist to infants immediately after Baptism, henceforward out of reverence for this august Sacrament, under no plea should Communion, not even under the species of wine, be given to children when they were baptized.[116] Benedict XIV forbade the Italo-Greeks to administer Communion to infants, but acknowledged that it was the custom among the Orientals.[117]

This custom of infant Communion gradually disappeared. In the Western Church the practice of solemn baptism on Holy Saturday had ceased almost everywhere by the twelfth

[114] *Sacramentarium Gregorianum*, (De sabbato sancto): "Qui etiam non prohibentur lactari ante sanctam communionem, si necesse fuerit."—*MPL*, LXXVIII, 90.

[115] S. C. de Prop. Fide, 5 apr. 1729—*Acta et Decreta Sacrorum Conciliorum Recentiorum Collectio Lacensis, Auctoribus Presbyteris S. J. e domo B. V. M. Sine Labe Conceptae ad Lacum* (7 vols., Friburgi Brisgoviae: 1870-1890), II, 442; c., S. Thomas, *Summa Theologica*, Pars III, q. LXXX, a. 9, ad 3; Benedictus XIV, ep. encycl., "*Allatae sunt*," 26 iul. 1755, Ad Missionarios per Orientem deputatos, No. 24—*Fontes*, n. 434.

[116] Mansi, XXXVIII, 108.

[117] Benedictus XIV, const., "*Etsi pastoralis*," 26 maii 1742—*Fontes* n. 328. (The Constitution "*Etsi pastoralis*" deals with a special problem of the Italo-Greek population in Southern Italy.)

century, and with it also the practice of giving Communion to the newly baptized infants.[118]

ARTICLE 3

THE EUCHARISTIC FAST AND LAY COMMUNION

Although all the Councils, with the exception of that of Hippo (393) and of the II Council of Macon (585), speak only of the obligation of fasting for priests celebrating Mass, nevertheless, the same law of fasting was clearly understood with regard to lay Communion. The reason given for the fast in the Council of Macon is common to both in this one respect at least, namely, it is not fitting that bodily nourishment should be esteemed greater than the spiritual food of the Eucharist.[119] Wherefore, it was stated in the same Council that children who were to receive Communion should be fasting. The Roman Ordos also imposed the fast even on infants who received Holy Communion after baptism. The Fathers of the Church likewise in their writings not only spoke of fasting preceding the celebration of Mass but also of fasting preceding the Communion of the laity.

Pope Saint Stephen III, writing to King Pepin deplored the excesses of the Lombards, who partook of the Eucharist, surfeited with food.[120] Pope Saint Nicholas I (858), too, in his reply to the Bulgarians strictly intimates the law of

[118] Cf. Benedictus XIV, ep. "*Quadam,*" 24 mart. 1756, ¶ 7—*Fontes* n. 439; Many, *Praelectiones de Missa cum Appendice de Sanctissimo Sacramento Eucharistiae,* p. 229.

[119] II Council of Macon, c. 6: "Ne spirituali alimento corporale praeponatur."—Mansi, IX, 952.

[120] Ad Pippinum Regem—Mansi, XII, 541; (Pope Stephen III [752-757] is sometimes referred to as Stephen II, since Pope Stephen II, who ascended the Papal chair March 27, 752, died a few days later. By reason of his short reign his name is frequently omitted from the lists of Popes.)

the fast for the laity.[121] The law of fasting Communion was likewise laid down in the *Decree of Gratian.*[122]

In the Decree of Burchard (eleventh century) the precept of fasting for the laity is clear, and moreover, a penance was imposed on those who violated the precept. This canon of the Decree is attributed to Pope Eutychianus, who reigned from 275-283.[123]

As early as the time of Pope Nicholas I, even the manner in which the fast was broken was discussed. The question was asked concerning blood coming from the nose or mouth. Was it to be considered breaking the fast? It was not. This answer already reveals some progress in the legislation of the law of the Eucharistic fast.[124]

The practice of the Eucharistic fast was so rigorous that the canon prescribed that those who received Communion in the morning were to remain fasting until noon, and those who received at ten o'clock were not to take any nourishment till sunset.[125]

Durandus, a noted canonist and liturgist of the thirteenth century, says that this ruling had already ceased in his

121 *Ad Consulta Bulgarorum,* cap. LXV: "Tunc recte non licet cuilibet communinoem Christi percipere, quando gulae deditus non invenitur ieiunus, adeo ut, mysticam mensam parvipendens, prius cibi laici sumptu ac pretiosum sanguinem a caeteris non discernens alimentis, non praeposuisse omni humanae refectioni, sed postposuisse noscatur."—Mansi, XV, 423-424.

122 C. 54, D. III, *de cons.*

123 Lib. V, c. 35: "Qui acceperant sacrificium post cibum aut post aliquam parvissimam refectionem, nisi pro viatico, pueri tres dies, maiores septem, clerici viginti dies poeniteant."—*MPL,* CXL, 759.

124 *Ad Consulta Bulgarorum,* cap. LXV: "Caeterum quam ob rem non debet is cui sanguis ex ore vel naribus profluxerit, corpus ac Sanguinem Christi percipere, regula nulla docet. Nam quod invitus quis patitur, in culpam ei non debet imputari ac per hoc nec a participatione tanti remedii coerceri."—Mansi, XV, 424.

125 *Decretum Burchardi,* Lib. V. c. 11: "Si igitur mane Dominica porrigitur, usque ad sextam ieiunent ministri qui eam consumperint. Et si tertia vel quarta hora acceperint, ieiunent usque ad horam vesperam."—*MPL,* CXL, 754. This precept is attributed to Pope Clement I, who ruled the Church from 91-100. However, it is not likely that this canon dates from such an early time.

time.[126] Soto on the contrary says it still existed in the fifteenth century.[127]

Furthermore, it was even necessary to be fasting to assist at High Mass even though one did not receive Communion. This custom was followed from the earliest times, and fell into disuse only in the late Middle Ages. In the *Capitula of Martinus* who was Metropolitan of Braga, at the time that the third Council was celebrated in that city (572), this law was already prescribed.[128] In a Greek homily which Zahn has edited and which he attributes to Eusebius of Emesa in the middle of the fourth century, the preacher makes out a sort of scale of offenses in the matter of Sunday observance. "If," he says, "a man breaks his fast before the public liturgy of the Church is completed, he is in danger of judgment, but if he takes food before Communion he is in danger of hell fire."[129] Pope Nicholas I, authoritatively declared that it was wrong for anyone to take food before the third hour (i.e., nine o'clock, the hour for the public Mass).[130]

In the *Capitula of Theodolfus* (eighth century), Bishop of Orleans, reproduced two hundred years later (994) in the *Liber legum ecclesiasticarum*, a similar abstention was insisted upon.[131]

[126] Durandus in 4 dist. 8, quaest. 4 num. 16 (quoted by Vasquez, *In Summa D. Thomae*, disp. CCXI, art. 7, cap. I).

[127] Soto, *Commentarius in Quartum* (*quem vocant*) *Sententiarum* (2 vols., Venetiis: 1575), dist. XII, quaest. 1, art. 8.

[128] C. 64: "Non liceat quemlibet die dominica ab ecclesia absentem esse, sed missarum solemnibus interesse et ieiunio."—(Browe, "Die Neuchternheit ver der Messe und Kommunion in Mittelalter,"—*Ephemerides Liturgicae*, XLV [1931], 229.)

[129] *Skizzen aus dem Leben der alten Kirche*, p. 284 (quoted by Thurston, *ER*, XCI [1934], 573.)

[130] *Ad Consulta Bulgarorum*, cap. LX—Mansi, XV, 422; MPL, CXIX, 1002.

[131] C. 39, c. 46—Mansi, XIII, 1005, 1006; *Liber legum ecclesiasticarum*, (c. 45): "Praecipimus igitur ut nemo cibum aliquem gustet, antequam servitium missae publicae impletum sit, sed omnes tam feminae quam viri congregentur ad missam magnam, et ad sanctam et spiritualem ecclesiam, et ibi missam magnam et praedicationem verbi divini audiant."—Mansi, XIX, 193; *Decretum Burchardi*, lib. II, c. 54—*MPL*, CXL, 655; Corblet, *Hist. du Sacr. de l'Euch.* I, 320.

In the beginning of the fifteenth century this usage was no longer insisted upon, as appears from the works of John Gerson (1429).[132]

ARTICLE 4

EXCEPTIONS FROM THE LAW OF THE EUCHARISTIC FAST

However, there were some cases for which an exception was made from the rule of not receiving Holy Communion after having broken one's fast. The first was when in imminent danger of death there was necessity of receiving Viaticum. A second reason was if a priest was taken ill and could not finish the Mass. Another priest, even though he was not fasting, was not only allowed, but was obliged to complete the Holy Sacrifice.

The third reason was the necesity of preventing irreverence towards the Blessed Sacrament. This was not so much an exception from the law, as a necessity that knew no law. The ecclesiastical law of the Eucharistic fast was introduced precisely to safeguard the reverence due to the Blessed Sacrament, and hence, ceased to bind when something was feared which would have resulted in greater irreverence, for example, if it would otherwise have been impossible to secure the Blessed Sacrament from profanation.

When one was sick, but not in danger of death, the law of the fast was still binding, because the law was universal. The exception made in favor of those who were in imminent danger of death was sanctioned by the universal practice of both the Eastern and Western Churches. Though we find no explicit mention of this exception in the early canons of the Western Church, yet from the fact that the necessity of Viaticum was insisted upon, it may be concluded that the ecclesiastical law of the Eucharistic fast

132 *Sermo contra gulam in Domincus I Adventi*: "An audienda sit Missa die Dominico ieiuno stomacho? Dico hoc pertinere ad honestatem, non ad necessitatem regulariter."—*Opera Omnia*, III, 907. (Quoted by Browe, 'Die Nuechternheit vor der Messe und Kommunion im Mittelalter."—*Ephemerides Liturgicae*, XLV [1931], 281.)

was foregone in cases where the Viaticum was to be administered. Thus the I Council of Nice ruled that with regard to those dying, the ancient and canonical law should continue to be observed, namely, if anyone be near death let him not be deprived of the last and most necessary viaticum.[133] An exception from the fast for those who received Viaticum was made in the Decree of Burchard (tenth century), and the ruling is attributed to Pope Eutychianus, who ruled the Church in the latter half of the third century.[134]

In the Eastern Church, a like exception was made in the canons of Timothy, Bishop of Alexandria (381-385), and in those of James of Edessa (687).[135]

Concerning the second exception, that of completing the Holy Sacrifice, the VII Council of Toledo (648), after providing that in case of the sickness of the celebrant another priest should finish the Mass, defined that no one should presume to use to his own advantage that which was granted *causa aegritudinis,* namely that no one should say Mass after having taken food or drink in the smallest quantity. Here again *quemlibet minimum* is stressed.[136]

[133] Schroeder, *Disciplinary Decrees of the General Councils,* p. 42. Though in the early days of the Church the word "Viaticum" did not have the restricted meaning it has now, but also included the *benedictio poenitentiae,* it did not exclude the reception of Communion, as has been held by some authors. Cf. Hefele, *History of the Church Councils,* I, 429; IV, 106.

[134] *Decretum Burchardi,* lib. V, c. 35: "Qui acceperint sacrificium post cibum. . .nisi pro viatico. . .poeniteat."—*MPL, CXL,* 759. The quotation is headed "*Ex Decreto Eutychii Papae,*" (275-283).

[135] *Resolutiones Canonicae Timothei Alexandrini;* "Nisi necessitas urgeat non licet edere quidquam aut bibere. . .neque nisi ex causa gravissimae infirmitatis, cum vitae periculo."—Many, *Praelectiones de Missa cum Appendice de Sanctissimo Sacramento Eucharistiae,* p. 326; cf. *Resol. Can. Iacobi Edesseni—supra,* p. , footnote 86.

[136] C. 2: "Ne tamen quod naturae languoris causa consulitur, in praesumptionis perniciem convertatur, nullus post cibi potuve (cibum potumve) quamlibet (quemlibet) minimum sumptum missae facere, nullus, absque patenti proventu molestiae, minister vel saceredos, cum coeperit, imperfecta officia praesumat omnino relinquere. Si quis haec tentare praesumpserit, excommunicationis sententiam sustinebit."—Mansi, X, 767.

Later the XI Council of Toledo (675), to avoid any occasion for abuses on this score, decreed that when the circumstances of time, place and the number of clergy allowed it, the celebrant should always have someone on hand to assist him, who would take his place if he could not finish the Mass.[137]

The rule, formerly declared in the Decretal Letter of Pope Soter (166-175),[138] and in the VII Council of Toledo,[139] that the Holy Sacrifice should be completed by another priest in case of illness or accident to the celebrant, was repeated in Gratian's Decree.[140] This precept was eventually introduced into the Rubrics of the Roman Missal.[141]

137 C. 14—Mansi, XI, 145; *Cf.* Bona, *Rerum Liturgicarum,* lib. I, cap. 21, n. 2.

138 Mansi, I, 691. (There is some doubt as to the authenticity of this decree. It is not to be found in the MSS. of Harduin.)

139 Mansi, X, 767.

140 C. 16, VII, q. 1.

141 *Missale Romanum,* tit. *De defectibus in celebratione Missarum occurrentibus,* C. X; *de defectibus in Ministerio ipso occurrentibus,* n. 3.

CHAPTER III

THIRTEENTH CENTURY TO THE CODE

Article I. Definite and Defined Legislation

The Councils, previous to the Decree of Gratian, were concerned chiefly with insisting on the necessity of the Eucharistic fast, especially for priests, prior to the celebration of Holy Mass. This was largely due to the abuses which continued contrary to the law, as was seen from the canons of the various councils. In the time subsequent to the Decree of Gratian only a few isolated instances of this same abuse are to be noted.[142] The legislation of this period is much more definite and detailed in stating the exact nature of the precepts of the Church in regard to the Eucharistic fast.

Innocent III (1198-1216) forbade any priest to take the ablutions at his first Mass if he was to binate.[143] Benedict XIV (1740-1758) recalled this point of legislation in his Epistle *"Declarasti,"* and again in reference to the celebration of three Masses on Christmas day.[144]

In some places the custom had prevailed for the pastor of two parishes to hold two services on Good Friday, first in the one parish and then in the other. That meant he was not fasting when he partook of the Presanctified Host at the second Office, as he had taken the unconsecrated wine at the first Mass of the Presanctified. The custom was condemned for that reason. To avoid this objection other priests of

142 Corblet, *Hist. du Sacr. de l'Euch.*, p. 321.

143 C. 5, X, *de celebratione missarum et sacramento Eucharistiae et divinis officis*, III, 4.

144 Benedictus XIV, ep. *"Declarasti,"* 16 mart. 1746, ¶ 6—*Fontes*, n. 365; Benedictus XIV, *De Synodo Dioecesana*, lib. VI, cap. 8, n. 2.

two parishes introduced the practice of saying the two Masses of the Presanctified, but in the first one partaking only of the consecrated Host. However, this too was proscribed as contrary to the universal rite of the Church.[145]

The early Councils of the Church had expressed the limits of the fast in terms of *cibus potusque.* With the exception of the Council of Selingstad (1022) none had stated the *terminus a quo* from which it was to begin. The terminology *a media noctė,* which is now used to express the starting point of the fast was first used by Saint Thomas.[146] Since the Roman day began at midnight, and the fast was not to be understood absolutely in regard to all time, but relative to the same day, therefore the fast in the Latin Church also began at midnight.[147] This must have been clearly understood by all, since it was established in the practice of the Church. However, Benedict XIV says that the origin of enjoining the fast from midnight is unknown. It is worthy of note, he adds, that in the eleventh century, when it was not yet the custom for the clock to mark the hours, the Council of Selingstad enjoined the fast from *cockcrow.*[148]

In the latter half of the thirteenth century Saint Thomas formulated the principles pertaining to the Eucharistic fast. He distinguished the ecclesiastical fast from the natural or Eucharistic fast, which consisted in abstaining from all food and drink of whatever nature, even from anything taken as medicine. The former admitted of what is theologically known as *parvitas materiae.* The latter did not, and was broken by taking any food or drink, even in the smallest possible quantity. However, small particles of food left in the teeth or drops of water remaining in the mouth after it was rinsed, if swallowed accidentally, were not to be considered as having been taken as food or drink,

145 Benedictus XIV, ep. "*Declarasti,*" 16 mart. 1746, ¶ 23—*Fontes* n. 365.

146 S. Thomas, *Summa Theologica*, Pars III, q. LXXX, a. 8, ad 5.

147 S. Thomas, *loc. cit.*

148 Benedictus XIV, *De Sacrificio Missae*, lib. III, cap. 12, n. 1.

but *ad modum salivae,* and did not prevent one from going to Communion.[149]

These principles of the fast as enunciated by Saint Thomas were incorporated into the Rubrics of the Roman Missal,[150] and a practical application of them made to cases which might occur in the celebration of the Holy Sacrifice of the Mass.[151] The terminology *media nox* was used explicitly for the first time in ecclesiastical legislation to designate the time when the fast was to begin. The expression *etiam per modum medicinae* was also added to *post cibum postumve.* The Rubrics of the Missal did not introduce a third way by which the fast could be broken, but it expressly added "even by way of medicine," lest the taking of medicines should be excluded by anyone from *ratione cibi et potus.*[152] Godfredus and St. John of Paris, for example taught that medicine was permitted, because it was taken not *ad nutrimentum,* but *ad sanitatem.*[153]

Likewise, exception was made for the completion of the Holy Sacrifice of the Mass after the Consecration of one or both species by a non-fasting priest if the celebrant was unable to continue the Mass, or if the priest poured water only into the chalice at the Offertory, and did not notice his mistake, until he drank of the chalice at the Communion of the Mass.[154]

149 S. Thomas, *Summa Theologica,* Pars III, q. LXXX, a. 8.

150 *Missale Romanum,* tit. *De defectibus in celebratione missarum occurrentibus.* The rigor of the fast is intimated in the words of the Missal "Si quis non est ieiunus post mediam noctem, *etiam post sumptionem solius aquae. . .*"

151 S. Pius V, const., "*Quo primum,*" 14 iul. 1570—Fontes, n. 135.

152 *Missale Romanum,* tit. *De defectibus in celebratione missarum occurrentibus,* c. IX; *de defectibus dispositionis corporis,* n. 1.

153 Suarez, *De Sacramento Eucharistiae.* disp. LXVIII, sect. 3.

154 *Missale Romanum,* tit. *De defectibus in celebratione missarum occurrentibus* c. III, *de defectu panis,* n. 5; c. IV, *de defectu vini,* n. 5; c. IX, *de defectibus dispositionis corporis,* nn. 1, 2, 3, 4. In relation to the exception made for the completion of the Holy Sacrifice one should note a rather singular case. A priest who while celebrating the Sacred Office of the Presanctified on Good Friday, was taken sick before he had consumed the Sacred Species. There was not another priest present who was fasting. However the Deacon of

Likewise there were some who would also make an exception for Masses that began after noon. The reference here is not to the Masses celebrated for the departed, which custom, as already remarked, fell into disuse in the thirteenth century, but to those Masses which in some places were, by special dispensation, celebrated before midnight on Christmas Eve.

Even in these cases the fast was strictly required from the midnight previous unless a dispensation had been obtained. The dispensation to say Mass before midnight did not of itself include a dispensation from the Eucharistic fast.[155]

A fast of some hours was also required previous to Masses that began at midnight or shortly thereafter. This fast was not required for the Masses of Christmas Eve, which were celebrated at midnight, but for those Masses, which were allowed at night in exceptional cases, v.g., on the occasion of a pilgrimage. Leo XIII (Feb. 26, 1885) granted the privilege of saying Mass in the Church of Lourdes immediately after midnight, with this restriction, however, that the priests celebrating thus must have abstained from all food and drink for four hours.[156]

the Mass (a Deacon in rank also), was fasting. The question was asked of the Sacred Congregation of Rites: 1. In such a case should the Office of Good Friday be completed? 2. Should the Deacon who was fasting supply, or should another priest who was not fasting? The Sacred Congregation replied that if the minister as Deacon is a priest and fasting, he should finish the Office. If he is only a Deacon in rank and there is not another priest fasting, the Office is to cease, and the Sacred Host is to be placed in the Tabernacle, to be consumed on the following day after the celebrant has taken the Precious Blood in the Mass of Holy Saturday. S. C. R., 8 mart. 1825—*Fontes*, n. 5848.

155 In a certain Ordo for the celebration of the Divine Office, edited at Rome in the year 1643, it is stated: "Missa huius sanctissimae noctis debet celebrari post mediam noctem; aliter sacerdos non celebraret ieiunus. Celebraturus ante mediam noctem ex privilegio, vel legitima consuetudine, non dispensatur in ieiunio necessario ad Missam; id est a pridiana nocte ieiunit, neque in Missa vigiliae sumat purificationem." cf. Benedictus XIV, *De Synodo Dioecesana*, lib. VI, cap. 8, n. 21.

156 Prümmer, *Manuale Theologiae Moralis* (8 ed., 3 vols., Friburgi Brisgoviae: Herder, (1935-1936), Vol. III, *De Sacramentis in Genere et in Specie*, 149.

In 1415, the Council of Constance, in its condemnation of John Huss, also proscribed the abuse of the reception of Communion without fasting.[157] This error is not to be found in the articles of John Huss as listed by Church authority, nor in the articles of Wycliff,[158] who was also referred to by Pope Martin V in his epistle *"Inter cunctos"*, after the forty-fifth session of the Council.[159] Nevertheless it was condemned in Constance as a tenet of theirs and the condemnation was expressly confirmed by Martin V, who presided at the last session of the Council.[160] The discipline of the Eucharistic fast, which had become general in both the Eastern and Western Churches by reason of numerous provincial and synodal councils, and by authoritative pronouncements of many popes, here assumed the character of universal law.

The canonical exceptions to which the Council had reference were undoubtedly those of administering Viaticum, the necessity of completing the Holy Sacrifice of the Mass, and the prevention of irreverence towards the Blessed Sacrament. Concerning the Viaticum, the Roman Ritual expressed the legislation of the Church precisely and clearly.[161]

A response given by the Sacred Congregation of the

[157] Mansi, XXVII, 727.

[158] Mansi, XXVII, 1207-1220; *Fontes*, n. 43; c. Vasquez. *In Summa D. Thomae*, disp. CCXI, art. 8, cap. 1.

[159] *Fontes*, n. 43; Mansi, XXVII, 1204.

[160] Martinus V ([in Conc. Constantien.] const. "In eminentis," 22 febr. 1418): "Quod licet Christus post coenam instituterit, et suis discipulis administraverit sub utraque specie panis et vini hoc venerabile sacramentum tamen hoc non obstante, sacrorum canonum auctoritas laudibilis, et approbata consuetudo ecclesiae servavit et servat, quod huiusmodi sacramentum non debet confici post coenam, neque a fidelibus recipi non ieiunis nisi in infirmitatis, aut alterius necessitatis, a iure vel ecclesia concesso, vel admisso."—*Fontes*, n. 44.

[161] "Potest quidem Viaticum brevi morituris dari non ieiunis. . . caeteris autem infirmis qui ob devotionem in aegritudine communicant, danda, est Eucharistia ante per omnem cibum et potum, non aliter ac caeteris fidelibus, quibus nec etiam per modum medicinae ante aliquid sumere licet." *Rituale Romanum*, tit, IV, c. 4, *de communione infirmorum*, n. 4

Propagation of the Faith makes it evident that not only were those in danger of death from sickness excused from the obligation of the Eucharistic fast, but likewise those who were in danger of death from an extrinsic cause, *e.g.*, soldiers going into battle, or prisoners condemned to death.[162]

However, those who were detained in prison, even though they found it difficult to observe the fast, were nevertheless bound by the law except in grave sickness.[163]

The Roman Ritual, prescribing the order of the baptism of adults, indicated another case where one might receive Holy Communion while not fasting. Blessed salt was placed in the mouth of the catechumen, by which the natural fast is broken. Having finished the rite of the administration of Baptism, the Ritual says: "Then if it is at a suitable hour, Mass is celebrated, at which the newly baptized assist and devoutly receive the most Holy Eucharist."[164] This is also evident from an Instruction of the Sacred Congregation of the Propagation of the Faith.[165]

162 S. C. de Prop. Fide (C. P. pro Sin.), 21 iul 1841: "Quid de christianis vel sacerdotibus propter fidem non solum ad carceres perpetuos vel temporales damnatis, sed ad mortem laqueo vel gladio subeundam? Potestne illis deferri Sanctissimum Sacramentum pridie, vel ipso die eorum executionis? Et nunc debet illis administrari tamquam Viaticum moribundis, vel tamquam communio ordinaria benevalentibus? *Resp.* Affirmative, et per modum Viatici."—*Fontes*, n. 4789.

163 S. C. S. Off. (Coreae), 5 iul. 1854, ad 1—*Fontes*, n. 926.

164 *Rituale Romanum, Pauli V Pontificis Maximi iussu editum et a Benedicto XIV, Auctum et Castigatum* (Turonibus: 1896), tit. II, c. *Ordo baptismi adultorum*, n. 15.

165 S. C. de Prop Fide (instr. ad Vic. ap. Tunk. Orient., 16 febr. 1806): "Sale a catechumenis, in collatione baptismi praegustato etsi ieiunium frangi videatur, adhuc tamen nullum dubium est, quin ad sacram communionem, suscepto baptismate admitti possint, imo vero debeant; ita omnino Ecclesia, in cuius potestate est a generali lege ieiunii ecclesiastici, ab ipsamet is inducta, qui extra mortis periculum sacram communionem recipere cupiunt in peculiaribus casibus dispensare, in Rituali Romano praescribente, ubi ritum tradit, quo baptismus adultis conferendus est."—*Collectanea S. Congregationis de Propaganda Fide* (2 vols., Romae: Typographis Polyglotta S. C. de Propaganda Fide, 1907), n. 687.

It is certain that a priest would not have been allowed to say Mass after having broken his fast, solely for the reason that otherwise the faithful would have been deprived of Mass on a day of precept.[166] A decision of the Holy Office reads that fear of scandal or wonderment on the part of the people would not justify a priest in saying a second Mass if he had broken his fast.[167]

Vermeersch thinks that the word scandal in the response of the Holy Office is used more in the sense of wonderment, and not in the theological sense of the sin of scandal.[168]

Formerly the general teaching of canonists and theologians was that a priest who was not fasting could not say Mass to administer Viaticum to one who was dying. Thus Suarez,[169] DeLugo,[170] Benedict XIV,[171] Saint Alphonsus,[172] Soto,[173] and Sylvius.[174] Suarez taught that even the Bishop could not grant a dispensation for a particular case of this kind. Layman would not allow a priest who had broken his fast to say Mass to procure Viaticum for another person who was in danger of death, but would allow him to say Mass to administer Viaticum to himself.[175]

There remain a few words to be said concerning the use of tobacco before the reception of the Eucharist. It was disputed whether or not it broke the sacramental fast. Benedict XIV, in his treatise, *De Synodo Dioecesana,* traces

[166] S. C. de Prop Fide, instr. 24 maii 1860, n. 19—*Fontes*, n. 4877; Cf. Benedictus XIV, ep. "*Declarasti,*" 16 mart. 1746—*Fontes*, n. 365; Benedictus XIV, *De Sacrificio Missae*, lib. III, cap. 5, n. 4.

[167] S. C. S. Off. (Vallisprat.), 2 dec. 1874: "Se per ragione di scandalo o di ammirazione si possa giammai celebrare la seconda Messa dopo la prima quando già e stato infranto il digiuno. Resp. Negative."—*Fontes*, n. 1034.

[168] Vermeersch, *Theologia Moralis* (3 ed., 4 vols., Roma: Università Gregoriana, 1933). Vol. III, *De Rebus, De Sacramentis, De Legibus Ecclesiae et Censuris*, 256.

[169] *De Sacramento Eucharistiae*, disp. LXVIII, sect. 5.

[170] *De Sacramento Eucharistiae*, disp. XVI, sect. 2, n. 55.

[171] *De Sacrificio Missae*, lib. III, cap. 12, n. 8.

[172] *Theologia Moralis*, VI, 287.

[173] *In Quartum Sententiarum*. dist. XII, q. 1, art. 8.

[174] *Commentaria in Tertiam Partem S. Thos.*, q. 80, a. 8.

[175] *Theologia Moralis*, lib. V, tract. 4, cap. 6.

the history of the question, from the time when it was forbidden under penalty of excommunication until it was declared unbecoming.[176]

The first Provincial Council of Lima (1582) forbade priests to smoke or to use snuff before the celebration of Holy Mass.[177]

A Provincial Council held at Mexico in 1585 decreed, that out of reverence for the Blessed Sacrament no priest or any lay person should make use of tobacco in any form before the reception of the Holy Eucharist.[178] This decree of the Council was promulgated by an edict of the Cardinal Archbishop of Seville in 1642 and the penalty of excommunication was pronounced against those who smoked or made use of tobacco within an hour before or an hour after the reception of Holy Communion.[179]

To understand this severe legislation of punishing such an infraction with a censure, it is necessary to recall that the custom of smoking was formerly the object of such reprobation that Pope Innocent X (1664-1665) and Pope Innocent XI (1676-1689) had forbidden it in the Vatican Basilica.[180] Pope Urban VIII likewise had pronounced an excommunication against priests of the diocese of Seville who smoked in Church and above all before Mass.[181] Benedict

176 *De Synodo Dioecesana,* lib. XI, cap. 13.

177 I Provincial Council of Lima, Aug. 15, 1582, c. 24: "Prohibetur, sub reatu mortis aeternae, presbyteris celebraturis, ne tabachi fumum ore, aut sayri seu tabachi pulverem naribus, etiam praetextu medicinae, ante missae sacrificium sumant."—Mansi, XXXVI, bis. 218.

178 "Ob reverentiam, quae Eucharistiae percipiendae exhibenda est, praecipitur, ne alius sacerdos ante celebrationem, aut quaevis alia persona ante communionem quisquam tabachi, picietive, aut fimilium, medicamenti causa per modum fumalis evaporationis, aut alio quovis modo percipiat."—*Concilum Mexicanum Provinciale, Celebratum Mexici, Anno* 1585, *Confirmatum Romae,* 27 *Oct.* 1589, *et postea Iussu Regis editum Mexici* 1622 (Sumptibus D. D. Joannis de la Serna, Archiepiscopi. Parisii: 1625, cum Privelegio Regis), Lib. III, Tit. XV, ¶ 13.

179 Benedictus XIV, *De Synodo Dioecesana,* lib. XI, cap. 13, n. 1.

180 Benedictus XIV, *loc. cit.*

181 Urbanus VIII, const. "*Cum Ecclesiae,*" 30 ian. 1642—*Fontes,* n. 222, ¶ 1.

XIII, however, permitted the use of tobacco in Saint Peter's Basilica.[182] The Sacred Congregation of the Council, previous to the time of Pope Benedict had advised bishops to remove this statute inflicting an excommunication on those who used tobacco in Church from their synodal laws, lest they incur the note of rigor.[183]

Some moralists had taught that the use of tobacco broke the natural fast. However, Benedict XIV was of the opinion that it did not. He admitted that there was some danger, when it was a question of chewing tobacco. But since the habit of smoking had become so general, and no longer gave offense or caused scandal, he considered the discipline of forbidding it under penalty of censure too severe, and counseled that it should be abolished.[184]

Article 2. The Communion of the Sick

By a concession of Pius X issued through the Sacred Congregation of the Council, December 7, 1906, persons who had been sick in bed for a month without any certain hope of a speedy recovery, and who were not able to keep the natural fast, but were forced to take some liquid food before Communion, were nevertheless allowed to receive Holy Communion once or twice a month if they lived in their own homes; once or twice a week if they lived in a religious house, hospital or place in which the Blessed Sacrament was habitually reserved, or which enjoyed the privilege of having Mass in a domestic Oratory.[185]

A Declaration of the same Congregation, approved by the Roman Pontiff, ruled that the term *decumbentes* em-

[182] Benedictus XIV, *op. cit.*, n. 3.
[183] Benedictus XIV, *loc. cit.*
[184] Benedictus XIV, *loc. cit.;* cf. also, Corblet, *Hist. du Sacr. de l'Euch.* I, 322.
[185] S. C. C., decr., 7 dec. 1906—*Fontes*, n. 4331; S. C. C. Romana et aliarum, 15 sept. 1906—Fontes, n. 4329; Cf. *ASS*, XXXIX (1906), 603-604; Cappello, *Tractatus Canonico-Moralis de Sacramentis*, I, 471-477.

braced not only those who were actually confined to their beds but also those who, because of the peculiar nature of their sickness, could not remain in bed, or those who were able to rise for a few hours each day, provided that the physician judged they could not keep the fast.[186]

From this Declaration it can be concluded that the circumstance that the sick person was actually confined to bed was merely accidental, since the infirmity was to be considered primarily and as a *condition sine qua non.* One person may be suffering from a much more serious disease, v.g., cancer, and not be able to remain in bed, than another person who can rest quietly in bed.[187]

Woywod considers this Declaration merely an extension of the original decree. "That the Sacred Congregation had doubts whether it was giving a mere declaration of the former decree, or an extension of it, is indicated by the phrase *facto verbo cum Sanctissimo.*"[188]

Per modum potus included broth, coffee or any other liquid food, with which could be mixed some solid, *v.g.*, a cereal or ground toast, provided that the mixture retained the nature of a liquid.[189]

The Decree of 1906 said nothing explicitly of the impossibility or the difficulty of keeping the fast. Cappello remarks that in the first two schemas of the Code drawn up, express mention of the impossibility of keeping the fast was made.[190]

186 S. C. C., 6 mart. 1907—*ASS*, XL (1907), 344.

187 "Ubi eadem est ratio, ibi eadem debet esse iuris dispositio."—Cappello, *Tractatus Canonico-Moralis de Sacramentis*, I, 474.

188 *A Practical Commentary on the Code of Canon Law* (4 ed., 2 vols., New York: Wagner, 1932), I, 411.

189 S. C. S. Off., 7 sept. 1897: "Mens est ut quando dicitur per modum potus significatur etiam quod permittitur usus iusculi, caffei, aliorumque ciborum liquidorum, cum quibus misceri potest aliqua substantia, uti, v. g., condita farina friatus panis, dummodo dicta mixtio non amittat naturam cibi liquidi."—*Fontes*, n. 1192. (This document is worded in Italian in the *Fontes*. The Latin translation is taken from *Analecta Ecclesiastica* (Romae: 1893-1911), VI, 142.

190 The first schema (can. 135, ¶ 2) read: "Aegrotis tamen qui cer-

Article 3. Dispensations

For exceptional cases other than those admitted by law, it was necessary to have an express dispensation in order to celebrate Mass, or to receive Holy Communion while not fasting. This dispensation was reserved to the Roman Pontiff himself. The first testimony of a relaxation of the law of the Eucharistic fast in a particular case was the dispensation granted by Pope Julius III (1550-1555) to the Emperor Charles V (1500-1558) in 1554, who later abdicated his throne, betook himself to a monastery and there gave himself up to a life of prayer. The reason for the granting of the dispensation was ill health. According to the Indult the emperor was allowed to receive Holy Communion after partaking of a small amount of solid food. From the account which is given by Pope Benedict XIV concerning this dispensation, it appears that the emperor was allowed to make use of the dispensation as often as he received Holy Communion, and that the dispensation was given *in perpetuum*.[191]

Pius IV (1559-1565) at the request of King Sebastian of Portugal, granted to some priests in India the permission to celebrate Mass even though they were not fasting, either because sickness or the inclemency of the climate made the fast too difficult, and at the same time, because of the small number of priests in the mission, they found it impossible to supply for the incapacitated priests.[192]

The same favor of receiving Holy Communion while not fasting was granted to Queen Elizabeth Christina, Queen of Bohemia, by Pope Innocent XIII (1721-1724), but only

tam spem non habent ut cito convalescant et naturale ieiunium in sua integritate servare nequeunt. . ." The other schema (can. 858, ¶2) read the same. cf. Cappello, *Tractatus Canonico-Moralis de Sacramentis*, I, 473.

[191] Benedictus XIV, ep. "Quadam," 24 mart. 1756, ¶11 & ¶12—*Fontes*, n. 439.

[192] Brief of Pius IV from the Secret Files of the Vatican—Benedictus XIV, *loc. cit.*, ¶9.

for the day of her coronation. The dispensation was given for reasons of ill health, and because the occasion demanded that she receive Holy Communion according to the ceremonial.[193] Benedict XIV granted this same indult to James III, the Pretender King of England, because of his age and failing health.[194]

These exceptions, however, were very rare, and a dispensation was granted only in most extraordinary cases.[195] Since it was a general law of the Church, bishops *iure proprio* could not dispense from it. They needed an indult or special faculties in order to do so.[196]

Since the Decree of Pius X on frequent Communion this dispensation has been granted more readily for those who could not morally keep the natural fast because of ill health. The mind of the Church was to foster devotion to the Blessed Sacrament, especially by encouraging frequent reception of Communion. Like a wise mother, the Church was ready to remove every obstacle that stood in the way of this devotion, while at the same time she took the precautions necessary to insure due reverence for this august Sacrament.

ARTICLE 4. THE RECKONING OF MIDNIGHT

In prescribing the fulfillment of ecclesiastical obligations which had regard to time, it was always understood that the Church followed the common usage in reckoning the hours of the day. This common usage was that which was accepted in any given place for civil life and ordinary busi-

193 Benedictus XIV, *loc. cit.*

194 Benedictus XIV, *op. cit.*, ¶ 13.

195 "In hoc praecepto ieiunii naturalis dispensare potest solus Papa. De facto autem neque ipse Papa dispensare solet."—De Lugo, *De Sacramento Eucharistiae*, disp. XVI, sect. 2, n. 55.

196 "Non potest episcopus dispensare in ieiunio naturali quia est praeceptum universale totius ecclesiae, et nulla auctoritate, vel consuetudine constat, datam esse episcopo facultatem dispensandi in illo. Per se autem inferior non potest dispensare in lege Superioris."—Suarez, *De Sacramento Eucharistiae*, disp. LXVIII, sect. 3, ¶ 5; Cf. *Fontes*, 439, ¶ 4.

ness. In the centuries before the invention of time-pieces, sun dials were used to determine time. This was known as apparent sun time. Later, time was calculated astronomically by the movement of the stars in the heavens. This is true time, but it was unsatisfactory for business purposes, because of the variation in the length of its days and hours. So it was decided to allot 365 days to each year. Hence, arose what is known as mean time. This time-unit, however, varied in different regions by reason of the variation of longitude. Consequently it was agreed to give up the old system of local mean time in favor of a standard mean time, which was called legal regional time, or zone time. This was eventually adopted by railroads, telegraph offices, and for public affairs.[197]

Since for the most part these times were fictitious time units, they did not always agree with true time. Yet they were in common usage, and in some places were legal time by order of the civil magistrate.

As a result the question arose regarding the use of time relative to the Eucharistic fast. Was midnight to be reckoned according to true time or could the legal time be followed?

At an earlier date, when the confusion resulting from the various kinds of time was not as great as it eventually became, the legal time of the place was followed.[198] Then by reason of various civil laws some difficulty was occasioned in determining the hour of midnight. In Naples, for instance, the government prescribed that all the clocks, with the exception of private ones, were to take the mean time of Rome in indicating noon. The result was that midnight in reality differed not only by reason of local mean time, but also by reason of the different meridian of Rome and

[197] Young, *The Elements of Astronomy* (Boston: 1892), pp. 33-36.

[198] Cf. Pasqualigus, *De Ieiunio, Praxis Ieiunii Ecclesiastici et Naturalis* (Genuae: 1665), decis. 444.

Naples. In some cases this difference amounted to more than a quarter of an hour.

Hence, the Cardinal Archbishop asked the Sacred Penitentiary: "If because of these circumstances, for the fulfillment of the natural fast and other ecclesiastical obligations, were the faithful in Naples free to follow the clocks indicating the hour according to the mean time of Rome, or were they obliged to follow that which the clock showed according to the true time of Naples?" The Sacred Penitentiary replied that the faithful were free to follow the mean time of Rome and were not obliged to follow the true time of Naples.[199]

From similar responses, one given by the Sacred Congregation of Rites in 1875, and another by the Sacred Penitentiary, it can be concluded that any of the three times, true, mean, or legal, may be followed in the observance of the natural fast.[200]

In order to remove the inconvenience arising from the divergence in local mean time, it was agreed in 1892, by the civil authorities to observe a legal regional time in all places within a certain area. To this end the earth was supposedly divided into twenty-four equal parts of fifteen degrees each, (starting with the Greenwich meridian). The space between adjacent lines constituted a time section, and corresponded to the time of one hour. Hence, all the places in the same section had the same time at one instant. In most countries this time was adopted as the legal ordinary time. It was commonly known as railroad time, and was followed as the official time in many, if not in all public offices. Since it was an arbitrary determination, it did not

[199] S. Poenit., 18 iun. 1873—*Fontes,* n. 6439; ASS, VII (1877), 399-400.

[200] S. C. R. *Clodien,* 7 aug. 1875, ad IX—*Fontes,* n. 6077; cf. Many, *Praelectiones de Missa cum Appendice de Sanctissimo Sacramento Eucharistiae,* pp. 45-46; S. Poenit., 29 nov. 1882: "Utrum ubi horologia adhibentur, tempori medio accomodata, ipsis sit standum. . . , tum pro ieiunio naturali servando, vel debet quis, aut saltem possit uti tempore vero." Resp. "Fideles in ieiunio naturali servando. . . sequi tempus medium posse, sed non tenri."—*Fontes,* n. 6434.

correspond exactly with true solar time, but varied according to the meridian where one was.

Therefore, it was again asked, whether the faithful in these places, where time was indicated according to the Greenwich meridian, could follow this zone time in the observance of ecclesiastical laws. The answer was given that the faithful were free to follow this method of calculation, but they were not bound to do so. Hence, they were at liberty to use any of the accepted methods of determining time.[201]

A few years later doubts were again had as regards the use of Greenwich time. Could it be followed even in those regions where *de facto* public clocks did not conform to the aforesaid time? This question was asked precisely relative to the obligation of the natural fast, since it was a matter of no small moment. The answer was in the affirmative. Even in such circumstances one was free to follow Greenwich time. This response was formally approved by His Holiness, Pope Leo XIII on the eleventh of August of the year 1899.[202]

In the polar regions, where the sun remains above the horizon for months at a time during the summer, and below the horizon during the winter months, there was apparent difficulty in reckoning the hour of midnight.[203]

There was no rule of the Church for such a case. The nearest approach to a decision in the matter was a resolution of the Sacred Congregation of Rites concerning the hour of the celebration of Holy Mass. An application of this resolution could be made relative to the reckoning of midnight, since the same reasons militated for both cases. To the doubt proposed regarding the celebration of Mass, the Sacred Congregation replied that the aurora was to be understood morally of the time which was equivalent to, and

201 S. C. S. Off., 27 apr. 1892; resp., datum a S. CC. S. Off., 9 maii 1892—*ASS*, XXXII (1899), 251-252; S. O. C., 22 iul. 1893—*Fontes*, n. 4287; cf. also Coll. S. C. P. F., n. 1842.

202 S. C. S. Off., 9 aug. 1899—*ASS*, XXXII (1899), 251-525.

203 Vasquez, *In Summa D. Thomae*, disp. CCXI, art. 8, cap. 21.

corresponded with the rising of the sun, that is from the beginning of the usual civil day, when men were accustomed to rise at dawn for work, according to the accepted and approved custom of the region. Hence, the mind of the Church was that in similar circumstances the time of the day was to be computed morally. Noon could have been determined either from the observation of the stars, or according to the brightness of the twilight. Once noon was determined, the other hours of the day could easily be fixed. For instance, midnight would occur just twelve hours later than noon.[204]

A SUMMARY OF THE HISTORY.

The origin and ancient discipline of the Church in regard to the Eucharistic fast is obscured by reason of the question of the *Agape*. We know from the story of the Last Supper that Christ instituted the Blessed Eucharist and gave Communion to the Apostles after a common festival banquet. A study of the exegesis of the texts of Sacred Scripture that treat of the Eucharistic liturgy gives no proof of the existence of a fast previous to the celebration and administration of the Eucharist in the Apostolic Age. Scripture rather seems to indicate that it was the custom for the first Christians to celebrate the Sacred Mysteries after a meal in common.

The first historical evidence we have of the existence of a Eucharistic fast, at least in fact, if not prescribed by law, is the testimony of Tertullian at the beginning of the third century. Throughout the course of the following centuries, references to the fast are more frequent, both in the Eastern and Western Churches.

Saint Augustine at the beginning of the fifth century testified to the universality of the practice of fasting before Communion.

204 S. C. R., Missalis Romani, 18 sept. 1634, 2 nov. 1934—*Fontes* n. 5304; cf. *ASS*, XII (1877), 399-400; Many, *Praelectiones de Missa cum Appendice de Sanctissimo Sacramento Eucharistiae*, pp. 49-50.

The earliest known enactment of any Council prescribing a fast previous to the reception of the Holy Eucharist was that decreed in the Council of Hippo (393). This ruling was confirmed by the III Council of Carthage (397). However, an exception was made by the latter Council for the evening celebration of the Holy Eucharist on Holy Thursday. On this occasion it was customary to celebrate the Divine Mysteries after an *Agape.* This custom became quite widespread. It was eventually condemned in the Trullan Synod (692).

Another usage which was repeatedly condemned as an abuse was the practice of celebrating *funeral Masses* in the afternoon without the observance of the Eucharistic fast. That this was a very ancient custom is evident, since it was proscribed by the III Council of Carthage (397). However, it continued in the Church for a long time, even till the thirteenth century.

The obligation of the Eucharistic fast was insisted upon not only for priests as a preparation for the celebration of Mass, but also for the laity prior to the reception of Holy Communion. It was also necessary to be fasting to assist at the High Mass. Moreover, a fast of some hours was imposed on the communicants after the reception of Holy Communion.

A mitigated fast was prescribed for infants, to whom Communion was administered after Baptism. Some Roman Ordos ordered a fast of only one hour, and at least one Ordo did not insist on a fast in cases of necessity.

This ancient custom of administering Communion to infants was discontinued in the twelfth century, but survived in the Oriental Church till the eighteenth century. The law of fasting for High Mass and after Communion fell into disuse in the late Middle Ages.

An exception from the law of the Eucharistic fast was made in favor of those who were in danger of death, or when there was necessity of preventing the profanation of the Blessed Sacrament. The VII Council of Toledo (646) also ordained that the ecclesiastical law of the Eucharistic fast was to be foregone when it was necessary to complete the Holy Sacrifice of the Mass.

It is not clear whether the Fathers of the early Councils understood the Eucharistic fast in the same sense as it is known in the present day, that is, in the sense of *total abstention from all food and drink from the previous midnight.* Tertullian expressed the notion of the fast in terms of "*before all food.*" The III Council of Braga (572) was explicit only with regard to the prohibition of *food.* The VII Council of Toledo (646) expressly *forbade all food and drink.* It also remarked on the stringency of the fast. A censure was pronounced against any priest who would dare to say Mass after having taken food or drink in the smallest quantity. The canons of the Eastern Church made exception for those who had broken their fast, if they had done so by taking *liquid food* only.

Nor is there any positive evidence that the early councils of the Western Church prescribed the Eucharistic fast strictly from the moment of midnight. In one or two instances we find the prohibition to say Mass for priests who had broken their fast after *cockcrow.*

Among the Orientals there was some disagreement as to when the obligation of the fast began. In some canons of the Syrian Church it was decreed that the Eucharistic fast obliged communicants from *sunset* of the previous day. In other statutes of the same Church midnight was designated as the *terminus a quo* of the Sacramental fast. An exception was also made if one had not broken one's fast after *dawn.* In this case it was permitted to receive the Holy Eucharist if one had sufficient reason, for instance, to receive Holy Communion on the occasion of a major feast day.

Subsequent to the Decree of Gratian legislation regarding the exact nature of the Eucharistic fast was more definite. Innocent III forbade any priests to binate after having taken the ablutions in his first Mass. Saint Thomas formulated the principles governing the Eucharistic fast. These rules were incorporated into the Rubrics of the Roman Missal, which was promulgated by Pope St. Pius V in 1570. The Rubrics expressly declared that the obligation of the fast was binding from midnight. The severity of the law was strongly insisted upon. Such expressions as, *even after having taken just water, even by way of medicine, in the smallest possible quantity,* can be observed. The Rubrics distinguished between what was taken by way of food and drink and what was consumed *ad modum salivae.* They also prescribed that if invalid matter was used for the Holy Sacrifice, and the error was not adverted to until the moment of Communion, new matter which was valid should be procured, and the Mass completed, nothwithstanding the fact that the priest had already broken his fast by consuming the invalid matter.

The Council of Constance (1418) decreed that the Eucharist must not be received after a repast, nor in any other condition except a state of fasting, outside the cases of necessity admitted by law. The decree of the Council clearly indicates that it was not introducing a new discipline, but merely confirming what the praiseworthy authority of the sacred Canons ordered, and what had been sanctioned by the approved custom of the Church. That is the first evidence of universal written legislation in regard to the Eucharistic fast. Among the canonical exceptions the Council had reference to were those of Viaticum, the completion of Holy Mass, and the prevention of irreverence towards the Holy Eucharist.

For exceptions other than these an express dispensation from the Roman Pontiff was required. The earliest known dispensation from the Eucharistic fast was that granted by Pope Julius III to King Charles V in the sixteenth century.

PART TWO

CANONICAL COMMENTARY

CHAPTER I

THE NATURAL FAST

Canon 808.—Sacerdoti celebrare ne liceat, nisi ieiunio naturali a media nocte servato.

Canon 858.—¶1. Qui a media nocte ieiunium naturale non servaverit, nequit ad sanctissimam Eucharistiam admitti, nisi mortis urgeat periculum, aut necessitas impediendi irreverentiam in sacramentum.

Canon 858.—¶2. Infirmi tamen qui iam a mense decumbunt sine certa spe ut cito convalescant, de prudenti confessarii consilio sanctissimam Eucharistiam sumere possunt semel aut bis in hebdomada, etsi aliquam medicinam vel aliquid per modum potus antea sumpserint.

Canon 808 rules that a priest is not allowed to say Mass unless he has kept the natural fast from midnight. And Canon 858, ¶1, imposes this same obligation on those who wish to receive Holy Communion, except when they are in danger of death, or unless it should become necessary to consume the Blessed Sacrament to safeguard it against irreverence. Paragraph 2 of this same canon makes an exception for the sick under certain conditions: "The sick, however, who have been *confined to bed* for a month without an assured hope of speedy recovery, may with the prudent advice of the confessor receive the Holy Eucharist once or twice a week, even though they have taken medicine or some *liquid food* beforehand."

The Church's law demanding a strict observance of the natural fast before the celebration of the Holy Sacrifice of the Mass and the reception of Holy Communion is of such a universal nature that it is difficult to conceive that it was ever otherwise. Yet a study of the history of the fast shows that this legislation has not always been uniform, but is rather a product of more or less gradual growth. This must not be construed to mean that the precept of the Church with regard to fasting before Communion is merely a late innovation on the part of the Church. Plentiful evidence has been offered to prove that to receive Communion fasting was an ancient and quite general practice in both the Eastern and Western Church. For centuries it has been urged with a stricter severity than is known in any other ecclesiastical discipline not involving validity. But in this, as in all other ecclesiastical matters, the Church's legislation was necessarily very much influenced by prevailing customs, conditions, and circumstances.

The practice of a Eucharistic *Agape*, which the majority of authorities believe to have preceded the Mass in the infant Church, would have precluded any possibility of a Eucharistic fast of any length of time. Moreover, it is evident what great difficulty would have accompanied the observance of a fast before the celebration of Mass and the reception of Holy Communion in the early days of the Church, when Mass was celebrated in the evening. Besides, during the time of persecution ecclesiastical legislation was necessarily meager. The Church was governed in good measure by tradition and custom, and most laws were of a purely local character. All this may explain in part the lack of a universal, written, and uniform legislation in the matter of the natural fast preparatory to Mass and Holy Communion.

Present day legislation expressed in the Code is substantially identical with that enacted in the Council of Constance in 1415, when it was decreed: "Although Christ instituted this venerable Sacrament after supper, and administered it to his disciples under the species of bread and wine, nevertheless, notwithstanding this, the laudable authority of the sacred canons, and the approved custom of the Church has ordered and does order that this sacrament should not be celebrated after a supper, nor should it be received by the faithful who are not fasting, except in case of sickness or of some other necessity granted or allowed by the law of the Church".[205]

In recent years Rome has devoted much attention to the subject of the Eucharistic fast. A decree of Pope Pius X, issued through the Sacred Congregation of the Council, provided that the sick who were confined to bed for a month without any assured hope of a speedy recovery might, even after having partaken of some liquid nourishment be allowed to receive Holy Communion, once or twice a month, or once or twice a week, depending on whether they lived at home or in some religious house. This was the first step towards a slight mitigation of an otherwise strict law.[206] Prior to that time the few dispensations that were granted in this matter were of such an exceptional nature, and even then given only for a very serious and public cause, that for all practical purposes the law was numbered among those in which the Church would not dispense. The letter of the Holy Office addressed to all the Ordinaries of the world in 1923 was an even greater concession. In it the Holy See declared that in certain circumstances, namely, when it was necessary for priests to binate or to celebrate Holy Mass at a late hour, it would be willing to grant them a dispensation whereby they would be allowed to take some liquid food, if the observance of the fast would otherwise entail a serious injury either to their ministry or to their health. For cases in which there was not time to have recourse to Rome, the Ordinaries themselves might grant the dispensation.[207]

For a better understanding of precisely what is enjoined by the law of the Eucharistic fast it becomes necessary to take the elements of the canon separately. The Code prescribes that the *natural fast* should be observed from the *hour of midnight* by all those who wish to say Mass or

205 Martinus V ([in Conc. Constantien.] const. "*In eminentis*", 22 febr. 1418)—*Fontes*, n. 44.
206 S. C. C., decr., 7 dec. 1906—*Fontes*, n. 4331.
207 S. C. S., Off., 22 mart. 1923—*AAS*, XV (1923), 151.

receive Holy Communion, with all due allowance for exceptions made by the Code itself, or by other competent ecclesiastical authority.

The Eucharistic or natural fast is to be clearly distinguished from the ecclesiastical fast. The latter prescribes that only one full meal may be taken in the course of the day, although it also allows a small consumption of food which in its quality and quantity will be regulated according to approved local custom; the former demands an absolute abstention from all food and drink beginning with the hour of midnight. Not every violation of the ecclesiastical fast is grave; but any infraction, even the slightest one, of the natural fast is always serious. This is the unanimous opinion of all ancient and modern theologians, and is stated explicitly in the Rubrics.[208] Hence, the opinion of one or two of the older theologians, who held that there could be a slight violation of the Eucharistic fast which would import no more than a venial sin, is to be rejected entirely.[209]

The nature of the natural fast is such that it is violated only when the following four conditions are verified:

1. That which is taken must be food, drink, or medicine.
2. The substance must be taken *ab extrinseco.*
3. There must be a true *manducatio,* i.e., the substance which is taken must be swallowed and transmitted to the stomach.

208 *Missale Romanum,* tit. *De defectibus in celebratione missarum occurrentibus,* c. IX, *de defectibus dispositionis corporis,* n. 1; S. Alphonsus, *Theologia Moralis,* VI, n. 278; S. Thomas, *Summa Theologica,* Pars. III, q. LXXX, a. 8; Tamburini, *Moralis Explicatio Iuris Divini Naturalis et Ecclesiastici* (1748), tract III, cap. X, n. 15; Benedictus XIV, *De Sacrificio Missae,* lib. III, cap. II, n. 96; Many, *Praelectiones de Missa cum Appendice de Sanctissimo Sacramento Eucharistiae,* p. 332; Cappello, *Tractatus Canonico-Moralis de Sacramentis,* I, 450; Prümmer, *Manuale Theologiae Moralis,* III, 149.

209 Pasqualigus, *De Ieiunio, Praxis Ieiunii Ecclesiastici et Naturalis,* Decis. 440.

4. This substance must be taken after the manner of food or drink, and not merely *per modum salivae* or *per modum respirationis.*[210]

If all of these four requisites are not verified in every case then it may not be said that one has broken the natural fast. The norm adopted to determine whether a given substance comes under the heading of food or drink or medicine is that of digestibility. The substance need not be nutritive, provided it is digestible.[211] In practice to judge whether or not a substance is digestible, one is to be guided by common opinion and chemical analysis. In cases of doubt the more favorable opinion may be followed, and when there is disagreement between what is held by common opinion and what is revealed by chemical analysis, the preference rests with the general consensus rather than with chemical science. Hence, if chemical analysis proves that a certain substance is not digestible, though it is commonly thought to be so, the consuming of such a substance will be regarded as breaking the fast; on the other hand, if chemical science shows that a substance upon consumption is convertible, while common opinion holds that it is not, the substance may be classed as non-digestible, and its con-

[210] La Croix, *Theologia Moralis* (2 vols., Coloniae: 1719), II, lib. VI, dub. II, art. 2; Many, *Praelectiones de Missa cum Appendice de Sanctissimo Sacramento Eucharistiae*, p. 331, sqq.; Cappello, *Tractatus Canonico-Moralis de Sacramentis*, I, 452; Vermeersch-Creusen, *Epitome Iuris Canonici*, II, 84; Prümmer, *Theologia Moralis*, III, 149; Davis, *Moral and Pastoral Theology*, (4 vols., New York: Sheed and Ward Inc., 1935), III, 212 ff.

[211] S. Alphonsus, *Theologia Moralis*, VI, 281; S. Thos., *Summa*, Pars III, q. LXXX, a. 8; where he says, "*Et ideo post assumptionem aquae vel alterius cibi . .non licet hoc sacramentum accipere, nec refert utrum aliquid huiusmodi nutriat vel non nutriat.*"; S. Albertus Magnus, *Opera Omnia*, in IV Sententias, ex editione Lugdunensi Castigata cura ac labore Augusti et Emilii Borguet (38 vols., Parisiis: 1890-1899), XXIX, dist. VIII, art. X; Cappello, *Tractatus Canonico-Moralis de Sacramentis*, I, 457; Davis, *Moral and Pastoral Theology*, III, 215.

sumption will not be regarded as breaking the fast.[212] This doctrine Vermeersch proposes as a probable opinion.[213]

An observation, worthy of note, before proceeding further with an explanation of what does and what does not break the Eucharistic fast, is the extent to which the intention influences in the observance or non-observance of the natural fast. It is difficult to assign a universal rule in this matter. To say that the breaking of the fast implies only a mere physical fact which can come to pass independently of the intention is not entirely correct. On the other hand, to say that the food or drink must be consumed consciously and deliberately in order to constitute a violation of the Eucharistic fast is even less exact. If the former assertion were true we could not explain how a thing which is purposely taken *per modum inhalationis* or *respirationis* does not break the fast. If the latter statement were correct it would follow that the Eucharistic fast would not be broken if one swallowed something accidentally or inadvertently, which is an obviously false conclusion. The nearest we can come to laying down somewhat of a principle in regard to this point is to state that as a general rule the intention does not influence in the act of eating or drinking, except in those cases in which something is swallowed *per modum salivae* or *per modum respirationis.* Hence, that which would not break the fast if it was swallowed unintentionally *per modum salivae* or *per modum respirationis,* would constitute a violation of the natural fast if it was thus consumed consciously and intentionally. For the intention would have the effect of making the mere physical act of swallowing something *per modum salivae* or *per modum respirationis* a voluntary act of eating or drinking. This principle can be more clearly demonstrated by an example. For instance, if a few drops of rain were accidentally swal-

212 *In dubio favores sunt ampliandi et odia restrigenda.* Cappello, *Tractatus Canonico-Moralis de Sacramentis,* I, 548; Davis, *Moral and Pastoral Theology,* III, 215.

213 *Theologia Moralis,* III, 322.

lowed *per modum inhalationis,* that fact alone would not break the fast. On the contrary, if a few drops of rain were purposely caught up and intentionally swallowed, that fact would be sufficient to break the Eucharistic fast.[214]

Among the things about which some question may arise, and which authors usually treat, are: metals, such as are made of gold, silver, iron, and lead; glass, stones, pebbles, clay, soil, wood, branches of trees, pits of fruit, finger nails, hair, resin from trees or plants, blades of grass, hay, straw, chaff, thread, wax, paper, and gum.

Metals when consumed do not break the fast or are not considered to break the fast according to the common opinion of theologians, unless they are chemically diluted or pulverized and then used for medicinal purposes, as charcoal tabloids, bismuth, sulphur, sodium, and iron geloids.[215]

Glass, stones or pebbles are not digestible and hence, if consumed, are not destructive of the fast.[216]

[214] De Lugo, *Opera Omnia* ([editio nova, 8 vols., Parisiis: 1853], *De Sacramento Eucharistiae,* disp. XV, sect. 2, n. 26, sqq): "An et quo sensu intentio influat in laesionem ieiunii? Ex iis quae tradidimus videretur denegandus huiusmodi influxus; nam ad rationem comestionis vel potationis nil refert utrum res cau an de industria sumatur. At contra, ut scite notat Lugo, 'multum refert intentio, vel casus, ut aliquis dicatur comedisse, vel non comedisse.' Sane intentio aliquando ita influit in actum, ut rationem comestionis vel potationis, qua secus careret, ipsi tribuat. Porro id contingit solum relate ad modum salivae et respirationis. Si quid enim cum saliva vel respirando ex industria seu intentione sumitur, intentio efficit ut cesset ratio salivae vel respirationis, et sumptio fiat voluntaria deglutio, i. e. vera propriaque comestio aut potatio." cf. Cappello, *Tractatus Canonico-Moralis de Sacramentis,* I, 457.

[215] S. Alphonsus, Theologia Moralis, lib. VI, n. 281; Sporer, *Theologia Moralis Sacramentalis in IV Partes Divisa* (3 ed., Salisburgi: 1711), p. 248; Billuart, *Summa Sancti Thomae* (editio nova, 9 vols., Parisiis: Sumptibus Letouzey et Ane,), De Eucharistia, dist. VI, a. IV, No. 2; Cappello, *Tractatus Canonico-Moralis de Sacramentis,* I, 458.

[216] Many, *Praelectiones de Missa cum Appendice de Sanctissimo Sacramento Eucharistiae,* p. 355; Davis, *Moral and Pastoral Theology,* III, 215; *Cappello, Tractatus Canonico-Moralis de Sacramentis,* I, 459.

Dry wood, dried twigs of bushes, dried pits of fruit (if cleaned of all pulp), finger nails and hair, since they lack all resin or sap, are not digestive or nutritive, and cannot be classed as food or drink.[217]

However, resin from trees or plants, and green wood or branches, are substances which when taken, do break the natural fast, since the juice is digestible. Likewise, blades of grass, straw, hay, and chaff are digestible.[218]

Whether or not thread, when taken, breaks the fast is disputed. Practically all authors distinguish between linen thread and silk or woolen thread. Some few do not make this distinction but affirm indiscriminately that the consumption of thread does not break the fast.[219]

Those who distinguish hold that the consumption of linen thread breaks the fast, but that the swallowing of silk or woolen thread does not, since the two latter are not digestible substances. Cappello calls this by far the most common and probable opinion.[220]

With regard to wax, practically all authors hold that it is digestible.[221] Cappello again distinguishes. If it is question of bees' wax or wax which is made from the fat of animals or from a similar substance, he thinks that undoubtedly the fast is broken by the consumption, because

[217] S. Alphonsus, *Theologia Moralis*, lib. VI, n. 281; *La Croix, Theologia Moralis*, II, lib. VI, dub. II, art. II; Prümmer, *Theologia Moralis*, III, 149; Cappello, *Tractatus Canonico-Moralis de Sacramentis*, I, 459.

[218] S. Alphonsus, *loc. cit.;* Many, *Praelectiones de Missa cum Appendice de Sanctissimo Sacramento Eucharistiae*, p. 335; Cappello, *Tractatus Canonico-Moralis de Sacramentis*, I, 459; Prümmer, *Theologia Moralis*, III, 149.

[219] Prümmer, *Theologia Moralis*, III, 149; Noldin, *Summa Theologiae Moralis* (7 ed., 3 vols., Oeniponte: 1908), III, *De Sacramentis*, 170.

[220] *Tractatus Canonico-Moralis de Sacramentis*, I, 460; cf. also S. Alphonsus, *Theologia Moralis*, VI, n. 281; Davis, *Moral and Pastoral Theology*, III, 215.

[221] S. Alphonsus, *Theologia Moralis*, VI, n. 281; Gasparri, *De Eucharistia*, I, 308; Noldin, *Theologia Moralis*, III, 170; Davis, *Moral and Pastoral Theology*, III, 215; *Aertnus, Theologia Moralis* (7 ed., 2 vols., Paderbornae: 1906), II, 266; Génicot, *Theologia Moralis* (2 vols., Lovanii: 1897), II, 235.

wax of this kind is truly digestible; not however, if it is question of wax which is known as paraffin.[222]

The more common opinion is that the fast is broken if one swallows paper.[223] However, Cappello says it does not.[224]

Small pieces of skin from the exterior of the lips or from the hands are commonly thought not to break the fast when they are swallowed, since they are ordinarily detached in such very small quantity.[225] Davis says that in the concrete case a penitent need not be deterred from going to Holy Communion because he or she has inadvertently bitten skin from the fingers.[226]

The chewing of gum of any kind, whether it is fresh gum, or gum from which the flavor has been extracted, breaks the fast. The chewing of fresh gum certainly does, since sugar is used in the manufacture of gum. Even gum which is not fresh seems to retain some digestive quality, since it is made from a vegetable substance that exudes from certain trees and shrubs, and which seems to be digestive.[227]

In the second place the substance must be taken *ab extrinseco,* because the very act of eating or drinking conveys this concept. Hence, one would not break his fast if, intentionally or unintentionally, he swallowed blood flowing interiorly from the tongue, the gums, or the nose, for the substance of blood in such a case was not taken from without.[228] The same cannot be said if the blood flows exteriorly from the nostrils, or from the outer part of the lips, unless it is in such minute quantity that it can be considered as taken *per modum salivae.* A thing is said to be taken *per*

222 *Tractatus Canonico-Moralis de Sacramentis,* I, 459.

223 S. Alphonsus, *Theologia Moralis,* VI, 280; Genicot, *Theologia Moralis,* II, 235.

224 *Tractatus Canonico-Moralis de Sacramentis,* I, 460.

225 Aertnys, *Theologia Moralis,* II, 266.

226 *Moral and Pastoral Theology,* III, 214.

227 Cappello, *Tractatus Canonico-Moralis de Sacramentis,* I, 460; Merkelbach, *Summa Theologiae Moralis* (3 vols., Parisiis: Desclee, 1931-1933), III, 230.

228 Suarez, *De Sacramento Eucharistiae,* disp. LXVIII, sect. 3, 4; S. Thomas, *Summa,* Pars III, q. LXXX, a. 8; Noldin, *De Sacramentis,* III, 170; Cappello, *Tractatus Canonico-Moralis de Sacramentis,* I, 452.

modum salivae when it is in such minute quantity that it is inseparably mixed with the saliva and swallowed with it. If particles of food left in the teeth are swallowed, they are considered swallowed *per modum salivae,* and do not prevent one from going to Holy Communion. There are some authors who make a distinction here between the cases in which one swallows those remaining particles purposely and the case in which one swallows them unintentionally. They would allow one to receive Communion if he swallowed these remaining particles unintentionally, not, however, if it was done deliberately, because, so they say, since it is done intentionally, it seems to constitute a new act of eating. Saint Alphonsus says this opinion is the more probable, although the negative opinion is not improbable.[229] This seems to be in conformity with the opinion of Saint Thomas.[230] Prümmer says this distinction is unwarranted, because the breaking of the fast is a physical fact independent of the will.[231] This reason is not valid in an absolute sense, since the intention may make a difference, as De Lugo remarks,[232] and Cappello admits.[233] A better reason would be that the Rubrics of the Missal do not make this distinction, but state in a general manner: "If the remaining particles of food left in the mouth are swallowed they do not prohibit one from going to Communion, since they are not swallowed by way of food but *per modum salivae.*" The compiler of the Rubrics was evidently aware of the fact that the making of any distinction was not intended for in the same number of the Rubrics, concerning another matter he does advert to a distinction by incorporating the

[229] *Theologia Moralis,* VI, n. 282.

[230] *Summa,* Pars III, q. LXXX, a. 8; Cf. also De Lugo, *De Sacramento Eucharistiae,* disp. XV, sect. 2. n. 36; Layman, *Theologia Moralis,* I, lib. V, tract, IV, cap. VI, n. 18; "*Non frangit ieiunium traiectio reliquarum cibi sive intentionaliter* (*quod certum est*) *sive etiam voluntaria* (*quod saltem probabile est*)."—Genicot, *Theologia Moralis,* II, 233.

[231] *Theologia Moralis,* III, 149.

[232] *De Sacramento Eucharistiae,* disp. XV, sect. 2, n. 27.

[233] *Tractatus Canonico-Moralis de Sacramentis,* I, 457.

phrase "*praeter intentionem.*" Besides, they are not taken *ab extrinseco* after midnight and thus pertain to a meal of the previous day. Moreover, insistence on this distinction would offer too great an occasion for many scruples and perplexities.[234]

It would not be a similar case if one were to place a lozenge or a piece of sugar or food in the mouth before midnight, and then swallow it after twelve o'clock. This would constitute the continuation or the completion of a meal, and would therefore be altogether different from the case in which merely some particles remain in the mouth after midnight, though the eating had ceased on the previous day.[235]

Thirdly, there must be a true *manducatio,* i.e., the food or drink must be swallowed, in order to violate the Eucharistic fast. The fact whether or not the food actually reaches the stomach is not to be too strongly urged. For it may happen that if only a very small quantity of food or drink is taken, it may be absorbed by the nutritive channels of the human system before it reaches the stomach.[236] Hence, if one only tastes a thing, without swallowing it, the Eucharistic fast would not be broken.[237]

Lastly, the substance must be taken in the manner of food or drink, and not merely *per modum salivae* or *per modum respirationis.* The words "in the manner of food or

[234] "*Si reliquiae cibi remanentes in ore transglutiantur, non impediunt communionem. . .Idem dicendum si lavando os deglutiatur stilla aquae praeter intentionem.*"—*Missale Romanum*, tit. *De defectibus in celebratione missarum occurrentibus,* c. IX, *de defectibus dispositionis corporis*, n. 3.

[235] De Lugo, *De Sacramento Eucharistiae*, disp. XV, sect. 2, n. 37; Suarez, *De Sacramento Eucharistiae*, disp. LXVIII, sect. 4; Prümmer, *Theologia Moralis*, III, 150; Cappello, *Tractatus Canonico-Moralis de Sacramentis*, I, 452.

[236] S. Alphonsus; *Theologia Moralis*, VI, 280.

[237] La Croix, *Theologia Moralis*, II, lib. VI, dub. II, art. 2; Sporer, *Theologia Moralis Sacramentalis*, Pars II, cap. VI, sect. 7, No. 2, n. 460; Layman, *Theologia Moralis*, lib. I, tract. IV, cap. VI.

drink" are to be understood in their natural sense, *e.g.*, in seeing a person rinsing his mouth or spraying his nose one would not say he was eating or drinking. Whatever is swallowed accidentally while breathing, *e.g.*, a few drops or rain or flakes of snow, an insect, or some such object, is swallowed *per modum inhalationis* and does not break the fast. However, if one intentionally opens his mouth for the purpose of catching up some drops of rain or flakes of snow and deliberately swallows them, he cannot then receive Holy Communion on the same day, for his intention renders such an action a true act of eating or drinking.[238]

Nor does smoking or snuffing tobacco debar one from going to Holy Communion. Even the chewing of tobacco is not incompatible with the keeping of the natural fast, provided the juice is not swallowed in great quantity. If only a small quantity is unintentionally swallowed, it is done so *per modum salivae*, even if some grains of the tobacco are accidentally swallowed along with the juice.[239] However, Saint Alphonsus and practically all authors speak of the unbecomingness of such a habit, unless there is some sufficient reason for it, *v.g.*, to clear the throat or nasal passages.[240]

Washing the teeth, or rinsing the mouth, or gargling the throat is altogether licit before Communion. There is no need to be overscrupulous about this, since whatever drops of water remain are inseparably mixed with the saliva and swallowed with it. Even if one or two drops of water are unintentionally swallowed before they mix with the saliva, the fast remains intact, since the water was not taken to

[238] S. Alphonsus, *Theologia Moralis*, VI, 280; Sporer, *Theologia Sacramentalis*, Pars II, cap. VI, sect. 7, No. 2, n. 467; La Croix, *Theologia Moralis*, II, lib. VI, dub. II, art. 2; Billuart, *De Eucharistia*, dist. VI, art. 4, No. 2; Ballerini-Palmeri, *Opus Theologicum Morale* (7 vols., Prati: 1889-1893), IV, 668.

[239] S. Alphonsus, *loc. cit.*; Gasparri, *De Eucharistia*, I, 307; Gury-Ballerini, *Compendium Theologiae Moralis* (9 ed., 2 vols., Romae: 1889), II, 225; Cappello, *Tractatus Canonico-Moralis de Sacramentis*, I, 455; Elbel-Bierbaum, *Theologia Moralis* (3 vols., Paderbornae: 1892), III, 107.

[240] *Theologia Moralis*, VI, 280; Genicot, *Theologia Moralis*, II, 235; Capellmann, *Medicina Pastoralis* (7 ed., Aquisgrani: 1890), p. 123.

drink, but to rinse out the mouth.[241] This is one of the two cases in which the intention influences in the act of eating or drinking. The other case that in which something is swallowed *per modum inhalationis.*[242]

The use of a nose spray before Mass or Communion can also be countenanced, provided one takes the ordinary precautions not to swallow any of the liquid.[243] Likewise there seems to be no serious reason why the inhalation of some medicament, such as menthol or powder, could not be permitted since it is not eating or drinking. In all probability this would be licit, even if the dry menthol was placed on the tongue to dissolve, and then the fumes inhaled, provided the dissolving menthol itself was not swallowed. If only a small quantity of the liquid was swallowed, it would be *per modum salivae,* and not in the manner of food or drink.[244]

Subcutaneous injections and nutritive clysters or suppositories, even though they are intended as artificial nourishment do not break the fast since they are not taken in the manner of food or drink. Formerly this was a much disputed question. However, the negative opinion is today the more common and acceptable.[245] However, artificial feeding through the mouth by means of the insertion of a tube or other device verifies all the requisite conditions of eating and drinking, and furthermore, the food thus taken is subjected to digestion. Therefore, in the case of artificial

241 S. Alphonsus, *Theologia Moralis,* VI, 279; S. Thomas, *Summa,* Pars III, q. LXXX, a. 8; Suarez, *De Sacramento Eucharistiae,* disp. LXVIII, sect. 3, 4.

242 Cappello, *Tractatus Canonico-Moralis de Sacramentis,* I, 457; Vermeersch, *Theologia Moralis,* III, 323.

243 Murray, "The Fast before Holy Communion," *Homiletic Monthly and Pastoral Review,* 2 series, XXV (1925), 977.

244 Ballerini-Palmieri, *Opus Theologicum Morale,* IV, 668; Harty, "Notes and Queries," *IER,* 4 series, XXV (1909), 307.

245 Cappello, *Tractatus Canonico-Moralis de Sacramentis,* I, 455; Prümmer, *Theologia Moralis,* III, 150, footnote 130; Capellmann, *Medicina Pastoralis,* p. 123; Genicot, *Theologia Moralis,* II, 234.

nutrition through the mouth the Eucharistic fast is broken.[246]

A more difficult problem for solution is the question of the licit use of the stomach pump, by which water is injected into the stomach and pumped out again, before Mass or Holy Communion. There has been much controversy on the subject. Some theologians do not allow the use of it under any circumstances.[247] Others permit it provided oil or any other substance is not used to render the introduction and passage of the tube less difficult.[248] These authors are in the majority. Some authors go still further and affirm that the use of the stomach pump in all probability does not break the Eucharistic fast even if the tube is oiled.[249]

What then, may be said about the use of the stomach pump? In the hypothesis that for the introduction of its tube no oil is used, does it break the fast? The Eucharistic fast is violated only when all the four following conditions are verified:

1. That which is taken must be food, drink, or medicine.
2. The substance must be taken *ab extrinseco*.
3. It must be transmitted to the stomach.
4. It must be taken by the action of eating or drinking.

[246] Prümmer, *Theologia Moralis*, III, 150, footnote 130; Cappello, *Tractatus Canonico-Moralis de Sacramentis*, I, 456; Davis, *Moral and Pastoral Theology*, III, 214.

[247] Gasparri, *De Eucharistia*, I, 308; Jorio, *La Communione Agl' Infermi* (Roma: Pontificia Libreria Editrice Pustet, 1931), p. 37.

[248] Many, *Praelectiones de Missa cum Appendice de Sanctissimo Sacramento Eucharistiae*, p. 336; Gennari, *Consultations de Moral, de Droit Canonique, et de Liturgie* (5 vols., Paris: 1907-1910), II, 501; Genicot, *Theologia Moralis*, II, 234; "Les Lavages de l'Estomac et la Sainte Communion," *Le Canoniste Contemporain*, XX (1897), 141; "Circo l'uso della pompa gastrica in ordine alla SS. Comunione," *Il Monitore Ecclesiastico*, IX (1895), 182-184.

[249] Cappello, *Tractatus Canonico-Moralis de Sacramentis*, I, 456; Coucke, "De Ieiunio Eucharistico," *Collationes Brugensis*, XXXIV (1934), 383; Murray, "The Fast Before Holy Communion," *Homiletic Monthly and Pastoral Review*, 2 series, XXV (1925) 976.

As regards the first condition: the water may be said to be drink, and of itself is sufficient matter to break the natural fast. Regarding the second: the water is taken *ab extrinseco*, though it may be observed that not every substance coming from without does break the fast.[250] The third condition is that the food or drink must pass into the stomach. This condition is fulfilled in the case. What about the fourth condition that the substance must be taken as food or drink? This condition is not verified in the use of the stomach pump. To eat and drink in ordinary language means to take something into the mouth and swallow it. But in the use of the stomach pump, no liquid is taken into the mouth; it does not touch the tongue or palate; it is not swallowed in the natural manner; it does not pass into the stomach in the ordinary way.[251] In a word, it is not taken to drink. It is not used for that end, nor for the purpose of artificial nourishment. This would also be true even if some few drops of the water remained in the stomach, since this is altogether unintentional.[252] Prümmer says this is a probable opinion.[253] The same principle can be applied as is given in the Rubrics concerning one who unintentionally swallows a few drops of water while rinsing his mouth.[254]

A question concerning the licit use of the stomach pump before the celebration of Mass was proposed to the Holy Office, April 23, 1890. The request was presented to the Holy Office by a priest, who on the advice of his physician made use of the stomach pump daily. At first he made use

250 Gennari, *Consultations de Moral, de Droit Canonique, et de Liturgie*, II, 501: Many, *loc. cit.; Le Canoniste Contemporain, loc. cit.; Il Monitore Ecclesiastico, op. cit.;* 184.

251 Gennari, *loc. cit.; Il Monitore Ecclesiastico, loc. cit.; Le Canoniste Contemporain, loc. cit.;* Coucke, "*De Ieiunio Eucharistico*," *Collationes Brugenses*, XXXIV (1934), 380.

252 Cappello, *Tractatus Canonico-Moralis de Sacramentis*, I, 456; Many, *Praelectiones de Missa cum Appendice de Sanctissimo Sacramento Eucharistiae*, p. 336; O'Neill, "A Case Concerning the Eucharistic Fast," *IER*, 5 series, XXVI (1925), 401.

253 *Theologia Moralis*, III, 150.

254 *Missale Romanum*, tit. *De defectibus in celebratione missarum occurrentibus*, c. IX, *De defectibus in dispositione corporis*, n. 3.

of it two hours after Mass, but because of an obvious danger of irreverence towards the not yet corrupted sacramental species, he petitioned the Holy Office that he might be permitted to make use of it before Mass. The Sacred Congregation answered: "The Holy Father is to be asked for the favor." The Holy Father granted the request.[255] The same kind of reply was given to petitions presented on July 3, 1909, and March 28, 1923.[256]

This reply is variously interpreted by canonists. Some maintain it indicates that the Eucharistic fast is broken by the use of the stomach pump, and consequently a dispensation from the ecclesiastical law had to be obtained in the case.[257]

Jorio's observation in regard to this reply of the Sacred Congregation of the Holy Office is: "At any rate the question of the principle has been left officially undecided, and this being the case, the question is still open to discussion: nevertheless, in practice, and in the spirit of the law, the responses of the Sacred Congregation of the Holy Office indicates that because of the subtlety of the argument, recourse should be had to the Holy See."[258]

Other authors say that the inference of a needed dispensation is unwarranted.[259] Here are their reasons: 1) The reply does not solve the theoretical doubt, since a theoretical doubt was not proposed to the Sacred Congregation but only a particular dispensation was requested. There was simply no decision made by the Holy Office, so that the question remained an open one, after as before. 2) Frequently

[255] *Il Monitore Ecclesiastico, loc. cit.; Le Canoniste Contemporain, loc. cit.*

[256] Jorio, *La Communione Agl' Infermi*, p. 37.

[257] Gasparri, *De Eucharistia*, I, 308.

[258] *La Communione Agl' Infermi*, p. 37.

[259] Genarri, *Consultations de Moral, de Droit et de Liturgie*, II, 501; Many, *Praelectiones de Missa cum Appendice de Sanctissimo Sacramento Eucharistiae*, p. 336; *Cappello, Tractatus Canonico-Moralis de Sacramentis*, I, 445; *Il Monitore Ecclesiastico, loc. cit.; Le Canoniste Contemporain, loc. cit.*; Murray, "The Fast Before Holy Communion," *loc. cit.*

the dispensations are granted to allay scruples or *ad cautelam.* Moreover, these authors observe that this reply of the Holy Office rather favors the opinion that the use of the stomach pump does not break the fast, for, if it were considered by the Sacred Congregation to be destructive of the fast, Rome would not have so freely granted a perpetual dispensation for a priest to say Mass while not fasting. The validity of this observation is more apparent if one recalls with what severity Rome was formerly accustomed to urge the observance of the Eucharistic fast, especially previous to the celebration of Holy Mass.

In 1909 the Sacred Congregation of the Sacraments for the purpose of learning the existing practice in such cases asked the Holy Office concerning it, and on the twenty-third of June received the following answer: "This Supreme Congregation, in 1890, at the instance of a priest who asked for permission to make use of the stomach pump before Mass, examined the question of principle of the use of the stomach pump in relation to the Eucharistic fast. Both questions were proposed, and the most eminent and reverend general cardinals inquisitors, without pronouncing further on the question decreed: *Pro gratia iuxta preces.* From this time forward, the same reply was given to similar requests."[260]

Evidently the Holy Office for reasons of its own did not wish to commit itself on the subject. From this last reply of the Holy Office it is obvious that the Sacred Congregation did not intend to solve the theoretical doubt, and the principle of the question remains open to discussion. A sufficient number of authorities who hold that the use of the stomach pump does not destroy the Eucharistic fast, makes it solidly probable that its use before Mass or Holy Communion is not illicit.

Hence, in practice one who finds it necessary to make use of the stomach pump may continue to do so, and feel sure

260 Jorio, *La Comunione Agl' Infermi*, p. 36.

that in all probability he is not breaking his fast. However, if anyone is preoccupied about it, he may ask for a dispensation which will not be refused him.

The discussion thus far has not been concerned with the licitness or illicitness of the use of the stomach pump apart from a grant for dispensation, when the tube is oiled. There seems to be no justification for its use in this case, since evidently some of the oil or preparatory substance adheres to the tongue or palate and is consumed in the manner of food. Being digestive it consequently breaks the fast when it is swallowed.[261] However, in a case wherein there is used some pure mineral oil that would pass through the body without assimilation, the oiling of the tube would be allowable, and the use of the stomach pump permissible.

When the stomach pump is used to introduce any other liquid into the stomach, such as milk or rose water, even though the liquid is not retained but immediately withdrawn by means of the tube, the fast is violated. For according to the common practice of physicians no other liquid than water is used for washing out the stomach. If other liquids are used, it may be presumed that there is the intention to supply nourishment to the patient, and not the sole intention of washing out the stomach. Hence, it is certain that in the case in which any liquid other than water is used to wash out the stomach, a dispensation from the Eucharistic fast is necessary for one who wishes to say Mass or receive Holy Communion after such a treatment.[262]

[261] *Le Canoniste Contemporain, op. cit.*, 141; *Il Monitore Ecclesiastico, op. cit.*, 184.

[262] Davis, *Moral and Pastoral Theology*, III, 214; Cappello, *Tractatus Canonico-Moralis de Sacramentis*, I, 456.

CHAPTER II

MIDNIGHT AND THE EUCHARISTIC FAST

The law of the Eucharistic fast obliges one to abstain from all food and drink from the previous midnight. While this obligation binds strictly from the very moment of midnight, yet the law giver has decreed that in the observance of the natural fast one may make use of any of the various times in the reckoning of the hour of midnight. The Code in canon 33, ¶1, reads: "In reckoning the hours of the day, the common custom or local usage of the place is to be followed, but for the private celebration of Holy Mass, the private recitation of the Divine Office, the reception of Holy Communion and the observance of fast and abstinence, though the usual computation of time differs, one may follow the local time, true or mean, or the legal time, regional or extraordinary."

Though the Code speaks only of the reception of Holy Communion, a choice of times is given not only in reckoning the hours during which Communion may be received according to the prescript of canon 867, but also in the reckoning of midnight, from which time the Eucharistic fast binds.[263]

This disposition of canon 33 is not altogether new in the Code of Canon Law. Previous to the New Code there were several decisions given by the Sacred Penitentiary and by the Sacred Congregation of Rites on the matter. These de-

[263] Michiels, *Normae Generales Iuris Canonici* (2 vols., Lublin: 1929), II, 138, footnote 2.

cisions explicitly stated that a choice of time was allowed in the observance of the Eucharistic fast.[264]

In order to demonstrate the application of canon 33, it is necessary to give a summary definition of the different kinds of time. The Code speaks of two general divisions of time: 1) *Tempus locale*, and 2) *Tempus legale*. Each is subdivided: the first into a) *tempus verum* and b) *tempus medium;* the latter into a) *tempus regionale* and b) *tempus aliud extraordinarium.*

Local time is the time of a certain place, and is determined by the motion of the earth in relation to the sun and stars. *True local time* is that which is measured, without any change or adaptation, from the apparent motion of the sun as it is indicated by a sun dial. It is frequently called *apparent time.* The length of a true solar day is not always uniform on account of the irregularity of the earth's motion around the sun. Hence, a solar day may be a little longer or a little shorter than our usual twenty-four hour day.[265]

Such an irregular time, which is manifestly inconvenient, is not accommodated to the necessities of civil life. Therefore, a *mean time* has been introduced to obviate the difficulties occasioned by the day to day variation of sun time. *Mean time* is a fictitious time unit, according to which all the days of the year are considered as being of exactly the same length, *i.e.*, of twenty-four hours. Since mean time

[264] S. R. C., Clodien., 7 aug. 1875, ad IX: "An tam pro recitatione Officii divini, quam pro ieiunio naturali ante Communionem praescripto vel etiam pro abstinentia a carnalibus aut lacticiniis diebus ieiunii, conformare se quis possit tempore dicto medio, ita ut aliquando uni, aliquando alteri adhaereat?" Resp. "Posse stare publicis horologiis."—*Fontes*, n. 6077; S. Poenit., 29 nov. 1882: "Utrum, ubi horologia adhibentur, tempori medio accomodata, ipsis sit standum. . . , pro ieiunio naturali servando; vel debet quis, aut saltem possit uti tempore vero?" Resp. "Fideles in ieiunio naturali servando. . .sequi tempus medium posse, sed non teneri."—*Fontes*, n. 6434.

[265] Michiels, *Normae Generales Iuris Canonici*, II, 128; Richarz, "Computing Time According to Canon Law," *ER*, LXXXVII (1932), 177.

is obtained by a scientific modification of solar time, it is obvious that there is a difference between the two. The difference between solar and mean time is called the equation of time. The maximum value of difference between these two times is sixteen minutes. However, this difference of sixteen minutes is had only when sun time is fast of mean time. The maximum difference when true sun time is slower than mean time is fourteen minutes.

The differences between a solar day and a mean day is not more than a minute or two. It is the successive accumulation of these minimal differences which in February makes the midnight of a solar day occur fourteen minutes later than the midnight of the mean day. In the beginning of November, when it is midnight according to the mean time the true time will be 12:16 A.M., while practically all through the month of February, when it is midnight according to mean time, the true time is 11:46 P.M. On all intermediate days the difference is less and it becomes zero on December twenty-sixth. In the summer months the deviation of the two times is less than it is in November or February. On the fifteenth day of May when it is midnight according to mean time, the true time is 12:04 A.M., while on the twenty-seventh of July it is 11:45 P.M. On the fifteenth of June the difference is again zero. True time in relation to local mean time varies according to the different seasons and days of the year, but not accord- to different localities. In other words, the difference between true time and local mean time on any given day is the same in all places, independent of their geographic position.[266]

The Code allows the faithful to follow either one of these times in the observance of the natural fast. As is evident,

[266] Michiels, *Normae Generales Iuris Canonici,* II, 129; Richarz, *loc. cit.;* World Almanac (1941), p. 165, which quotes as its source the United States Naval Observatory; Coucke, "De Ieiunio Eucharistico," *Collationes Brugensis,* XXXIV (1934), 380-386; Mitchell, "True Sun Time", *ER,* XC (1934), 80-81.

the computation of the difference between true time and local mean time is so very complicated that the liberty which is given by the Code to make use of true time is hardly of any practical value unless one has a knowledge of astronomy, or unless one has recourse to astronomical charts or calendars, which accurately indicate the difference of time between *tempus verum* and *tempus medium*.

Of more practical value is the rule of canon 33 which gives us a choice of following *legal regional time* (standard time), or *legal extraordinary time* (daylight saving time).

Regional time is that time which was introduced by a general agreement, whereby the Greenwich meridian in England was established as the prime meridian in relation to which time was to be counted. According to this manner of computation each unit of time which comprises approximately fifteen degrees of longitude is made the equivalent of one hour's time. All the places in each zone use, instead of their own local time, the time counted from the transit of the mean sun across the meridian which passes through the approximate center of that zone.[267]

In the United States there are four such standard time zones. These time zones are designated as Eastern, Central, Mountain, and Pacific, and the time in these zones is reckoned from the seventy-fifth, ninetieth, one hundred and fifth, and one hundred and twentieth meridian west of Greenwich. By the adoption of regional or standard time every fifteenth degree of longitude east or west of Greenwich and every multiple thereof are used as the central meridian for a given time belt. Therefore all places within seven degrees, thirty minutes, east and west of that me-

[267] Cf. *World Almanac* (1941), p. 165, which quotes as its source the United States Bureau of Standards. This time has been used in the United States since 1883. However, no legislative action for the country as a whole is recorded until 1918, when Congress directed the Interstate Commerce Commission to establish limits for the various time zones in this country.

ridian use the time counted from the transit of the mean sun across the central meridian. Thus Eastern Standard Time is identical with the local mean time of the seventy-fifth degree of longitude, and is five hours later than Greenwich time. This means that all the places which lie between sixty-seven degrees, thirty minutes, and eighty-two degrees, thirty minutes longitude, follow the same regional time.

The general rule is: if your place is east of the central standard meridian, your local midnight is earlier than the midnight by your clock (standard time), and you are not allowed to eat after midnight if you intend to keep the natural fast. If your place is west of the central standard meridian your local midnight is later than the midnight of your clock (standard time). In this case if you follow local time as the more favorable you may eat after midnight.

To ascertain the difference between local mean time and standard time the following rule can be applied: Look up on a geographic map the longitude of your place. Find the difference between the longitude of your place and that of the central standard meridian. Multiply this difference by four in order to get the difference in time (one degree equals four minutes). For parts of a degree it must be remembered that a quarter degree, or fifteen arc minutes, is equal to one time minute. For example, Washington, D.C., is on the seventy-seventh degree of longitude and therefore lies west of the central meridian. Seventy-five (the longitude of the central meridian) subtracted from seventy-seven equals two. Four times two is eight. Hence, when the clocks at Washington show midnight the local mean time is 11:52 P.M. according to local mean time. Consequently in Washington one may always, by making use of the difference between local mean time and standard time, avail himself of the privilege of eating or drinking until eight minutes after twelve, and yet be able to go to Holy Communion or to say Mass the following morning. On the other hand the longitude of New York is seventy-four degrees, *i.e.*, one degree east of the central meridian. Therefore, when the clock shows midnight, it is already four minutes after twelve by local mean time.[268]

Legal extraordinary time is that time which is introduced by the legislative authority of certain countries for some special or particular reason. Such is the summer time which is known in the United States as daylight saving time. Daylight saving time means advancing the clock by one hour. Hence, when it is one o'clock daylight saving time, it is only midnight standard time. However, it is to be noted that daylight saving time may not be made use of for the observance of the Eucharistic fast in those places where daylight saving time is not adopted as the legal time.[269]

According to the ruling of the first paragraph of canon 33, one is allowed to use one or the other of the various times mentioned in this same canon in the fulfillment of these ecclesiastical precepts, namely, for the celebration of private Mass, for the private recitation of the Divine Office, for the observance of the Eucharistic fast and the reception of Holy Communion, and for the law of fast and abstinence. Since this is a right granted by the Code, one can make use of the time which is most to his advantage. Hence, there is no doubt that it is lawful for one to say Mass or to receive Holy Communion, *e.g.*, on Sunday morning, although he or she has eaten between twelve and one o'clock daylight saving time from Saturday night to Sunday morning.. It

[268] *Cf.* Mitchell, "True Sun Time," *ER*, XC (1934), 81, where he gives an astonomical table showing the deviation of time between standard time and true sun time in various cities of the Eastern zone in the United States; *Cf.* also Mitchell, "What Time Is It? Midnight and Fasting," *ER*, LXXXIV (1931), 491-500.

[269] Michiels, *Normae Generales Iuris Canonici*, II, 131; Van Hove, Vol. I, *De Consuetudine, de Temporis Supputatione* (Romae: Dessain, 1933), 253.

is no less certain that one may eat after midnight daylight saving time on Friday night.[270]

However, canonists do not agree whether one may make use of a double reckoning of time. For example, may the same person eat meat after twelve o'clock daylight saving time and then receive Holy Communion the following morning? There are some who hold that a choice of time once made must remain the same for all precepts which are to be fulfilled simultaneously or consecutively. Toso and Maroto say that it is never allowed to adopt different times for different precepts if one and the same act is required at the same time for the fulfillment of a double precept. Both give the example of one who eats meat on Friday from twelve to one daylight saving time and then receives Holy Communion under the pretext that it was not yet midnight according to solar time.[271]

The *L'Ami du Clergé* absolutely rejects any conjunctive choice of two times as regards two precepts to be observed simultaneously or consecutively, and strongly assails the opinion of those who admit that a double choice of time is licit in the fulfillment of different obligations which bind simultaneously or consecutively. It proposes the same case. The author of the article says that there is no doubt that

270 Michiels, *loc. cit.;* Van Hove, *loc. cit.;* Woywod, "Daylight Saving Time and the Obligations in Which the Point of Time Is Important," *Homiletic Monthly and Pastoral Review*, 2 series, XXXVII (1927), 962-964.

271 Toso, *Commentaria Minora ad Codicem Iuris Canonici* (Città de Castello: 1921), p. 104: "Potest sequi (tempus quodlibet) libere et indiscriminatim dum ne ex duplici supputatione actus perficiantur, qui unica perfici non potusiset."; Moroto, *Institutiones Iuris Canonici* (3 ed., Romae: apud "Commentarium pro Religiosis"), I, 281: "Et licet modo unum sequi, modo aliud; . . .dummodo tamen unicus actus non urgeatur ad duas simul materias vel effectus obtinendos, quorum unus et alter diversum tempus exigerent; prout theologi moralistae dicunt non licere simul uti duplici probabilitate non existentiae duplicis praecepti, cum certa est alterutrius transgressio. Ita media nocte inter feriam sextam et sabbatum, si iuxta unum tempus hora duodecima iam fuerit elapsa, iuxta aliud vero tempus nondum sit expleta, minime liceret cuipiam carnes manducare quasi iam esset ille in sabbato, et deinde ad communionem accedere quasi in sabbato non manducasset."

such a pretext is erroneous. Here is his solution: "All is possible save the impossible. But a contradiction is impossible. And in this case the interpretation of the priest in question was a manifest contradiction. The astronomical hour comprised between midnight and one o'clock may indifferently, according to one's choice, be regarded as the last hour of Friday or the first hour of Saturday, but truly it cannot be accepted as being both at the same time."[272]

Cicognani says that though we can choose now one and again another time for satisfying divers precepts, yet this rule cannot be extended in such wise that a double reckoning of time can render those acts licit, which simultaneously under a single reckoning would not be licit. He observes that it is also the teaching of moralists that it is not licit to use a double probability regarding the non-existence of a twofold precept, when it is certain that this entails the transgression of one or the other.[273] Ojetti is of practically the same opinion.[274]

On the other hand, a great number of authorities do not distinguish between the cases in which one makes use of different times for divers obligations, whether or not these obligations must be fulfilled simultaneously or consecutively. In either case they allow the use of any of the various computations of time, provided that it is a question of specifically divers precepts.[275]

[272] "Questions de Science Ecclésiastique," *L'Ami du Clergé*, XXXIX (1922), 636; XL (1923), 200-203.

[273] *Canon Law*, (2 ed., Philadelphia: The Dolphin Press, 1935), p. 680.

[274] *Commentarium in Codicem Iuris Canonici* (4 vols., Romae: apud Aedes Universitatis Gregorianae, 1927-1931), I, 197: "Quare etsi conceptus ieiunii ecclesiastici et ieiunii eucharistici diversi sunt, coniungendi sent in aestimatione diei, quoties secus alterutrius legis violatio incurreretur."

[275] Vermeersch, *Theologia Moralis*, I, 357; Vermeersch-Creusen, *Epitome Iuris* Canonici, I, 138; Creusen, "Minuit Canonique" ou "Loi Pure et Simple," *Revue Théologique*, L. (1923), 464-474; Cocchi *Commentarium in Codicem Iuris Canonici*, Vol. I, *Normae Generales*, (5 ed., Torino: Marietti, 1938), 231; Coronata, *Compendium Iuris Canonici* (2 vols., Taurini: Marietti, 1937-1938), I, 161, footnote 3;

In general, the arguments upon which those who hold that we may at the same time make simultaneous use of different reckonings of time for divers precepts are the following: 1) the Code authorizes the use of the various times without making any distinction, and without setting any restriction on this usage; 2) Such a usage does not imply any contradiction; 3) This interpretation is not contrary to the authoritative responses concerning this matter which were given previous to the Code by the Sacred Congregations.

To make use of two or more kinds of time simultaneously for the fulfillment of divers obligations is certainly not opposed to ecclesiastical tradition. This is evident from the responses given by the Sacred Penitentiary and the Sacred Congregation of Rites. In these responses there is no indication that when one has chosen one specific reckoning of time he must then follow that same computation for all other precepts.[276]

Van Hove, *De Consuetudine, de Temporis Supputatione*, 260-264; Chelodi, *Ius de Personis* (editio altera a Bertagnolli aucta, Trento: Liberia Moderna di a A. Ardesi, 1926), p. 159; De Meester, *Compendium Iuris Canonici* (ed. nova, 3 vols. in 4, Brugia: 1921-1928), I, 191; Ferland, "L'Avance de l'Heure et Certains Préceptes de l'Eglise," *Semaine Religieuse de Québec*, XXXV (1923), 280-283, 567-570; 600-605, 614-121; Michiels, *Normae Generales Iuris Canonici*, II, 148; Eichman, *Lehrbuch des Kirchenrechts* (2 ed., Paderborn: Druck & Verlag von Ferdinand Schoningh, 1926), p. 44.

[276] Dubim propositum ad S. C. S. Off., 27 apr. 1892: "An liceat pro ieiunio naturali, quod signant tantum horologia viarum ferrearum etc., minime vero alia publica horologia? Resp. datum, 9 maii 1892: Affirmative ad primam partem, negative ad secundam partem.—*ASS*, XXXII (1899), 251-252; S. C. S. Off., 9 aug. 1899: "Utrum non obstante quod de facto non multis in locis alia horologia publica se conformarunt tempori medio Greenwich, clericis et fidelibus in Neerlandia in ieiunio naturali ceterisque obligationibus servandis, licitum sit sequi tempus illud medium Greenwich, quod inde a prima die mensis maii 1892 per totam Neerlandiam in omnibus officiis publicis tam viarum ferrearum, quam litterarum et telegrammatum expediendarum introductum fuit?

In Congregatione Generali S. R. et E. Inquisitionis ab Emis ac Rmis DD. Cardinalibus Generalibus Inquisitionibus habita, relato supradicto dubio, praehabitoque RR. DD. Consultorum voto, Emi ac Rmi Patres respondendum decreverunt: Affirmative.—*ASS*, XXXII (1899), 252; Cf. *supra*, S. R. C., *Clodien.*, 7 aug. 1875, ad IX—*Fontes*, n. 6077; S. Poenit., 29 nov. 1882—*Fontes*, n. 6434

Nor is the simultaneous choice of a double reckoning of time opposed to the universal teaching of moralists and canonists. While there are some authors who deny that the Code grants this option of choosing different times for the fulfillment of various precepts, yet the authorities in favor of such a use of time are in the majority, and the reasons given by them are more convincing.

A solution to the problem must be sought in an interpretation of canon 33. It was certainly intended by the Code to give the people the benefit of the difference of the various kinds of time. The Code grants this option without any indication that it intends to limit the freedom of making use of the various times in the fulfillment of divers precepts. Where the law does not distinguish, no distinction should be made.[277]

The interpretation of any law must be such that it does not defeat its own purpose. Such a defeat of the very purpose of the law would, of course, be manifest if one were to employ two separate computations of time in relation to a positive precept for the sake of lengthening the alloted period of time during which it can and must be fulfilled, or also in relation to a negative precept for the sake of shortening the assigned temporal duration during which it must be obeyed. To employ such an option would of course involve an evident contradiction. It can not be consistent in one and the same matter at one and the same time to anticipate or postpone the point of midnight which stands already determined by one's previous choice relative to its temporal fixation. Thus when one has anticipated his office with the earliest possible computation of time, he may not on the following day use a later computation at midnight for its ultimate completion. In like maner, it would not be lawful to begin Friday's abstinence according to standard time, and then to eat meat at twelve o'clock day-

[277] Vermeersch, *Theologia Moralis*, I, 352; Van Hove *De Consuetudine, de Temporis Supputatione*, p. 262.

light saving time on Friday night. Both these obligations which bind for a fixed period of time would wrongfully be lengthened for the fulfillment of the positive obligation and just as wrongfully shortened for compliance with the negative obligation. In a word, such a procedure could not be considered law-abiding, precisely because it would be undertaken outside of the temporal limits within the duration of which the obligation must be fulfilled as a positive precept, or at least remains binding as a negative precept.[278]

However, one may use two different times simultaneously when there is question of the observance of two different precepts. There is no inconsistency in eating after midnight according to one manner of time-reckoning and then saying Mass or going to Holy Communion in the morning, if according to any of the various computations of time mentioned in canon 33 of the Code it was not yet midnight. One could even eat meat on Friday night between midnight and 1:00 A.M. daylight saving time, and still receive Holy Communion on Saturday morning. In this case there are two different precepts, namely, abstaining from meat on Friday, and fasting for Mass or Communion on Saturday. These two precepts are not necessarily connected with or dependent on each other. There is merely a material and accidental concurrence of the two laws. Hence, we may make use of different reckonings of time in their fulfillment.[279] This is a natural consequence of the permission to follow any allowable computation of time. It is a question of various obligations.

The Eucharistic and the ecclesiastical fast are two different things, and can consequently be considered apart. Why should they have to be considered as one in the reckoning of the time of day? There is no intrinsic argument showing that they have to be considered as one. At most it might

278 Van Hove, *op. cit.*, p. 265; Woywod, "Daylight Saving Time and the Obligations in Which the Point of Time Is Important," *Homiletic Monthly and Pastoral Review*, 2 series, XXXVII (1937), 964.

279 Michiels, *Normae Generales Iuris Canonici*, II, 148.

be said: On account of the material affinity of both cases, and on account of the inconvenience that might arise, it must be presumed that the reasonable mind of the legislator is that they should be considered as one. However, this is a weak argument and has little or no objective juridical value. Actions formally different and precepts specifically distinct may be regulated at the same time by different laws. It is not additionally required that the fulfillment of the specifically distinct precepts eventuate in numerically distinct material actions before they may be regulated by different laws.[280]

Vermeersch, in commenting on the contents of canon 33, observes: Things must be considered in the light of *favorabilia* when the law itself permits a varying choice in the computation of time. It seems that in making this arrangement, the legislator has introduced for these different acts and duties a *common* time between the two days or two parts of a day, which *common* time may be considered either as part of the one or of the other day. Hence, there is nothing to prevent one from reciting his breviary according to true time, from observing the law of abstinence according to mean time, and from keeping the Eucharistic fast according to legal time.[281]

There seems to be no objection to such a practice, for in the case of reciting the Divine Office, of observing the law of abstinence, and of keeping the Eucharistic fast, the priest uses the difference of time in different ways, that is, with relation to different obligations. The Eucharistic and the ecclesiastical fasts are not one and the same, but really two distinct acts, in as far as there are two distinct formalities within the same material action. To consider the same hour as part of Friday and at the same time as part of Saturday admittedly implies a contradiction only then when one and also numerically the same obligation is dealt with. But when

280 Vermeersch-Creusen, *Epitome Iuris Canonici*, I, 138.
281 *Theologia Moralis*, I, 352.

the same hour is considered as part of two different days from the viewpoint of separate obligations, and therefore from specifically distinct aspects, no contradiction is involved.[282]

A contradiction is the affirmation and the negation of one and the same thing under one and the same respect. In the case in which one eats meat between twelve o'clock midnight and 1:00 A.M. daylight saving time, because it is no longer Friday, and then says Mass the morning following, because according to standard time his eating did not take place on Saturday, he indeed affirms at the same time that his act of eating was associated with both Friday and Saturday, but only according to different computations of time, and in regard to two divers obligations, which at most have only an accidental concurrence.[283]

The option of a double reckoning of time for different precepts is not opposed to theological tradition. The array of theologians and canonists in favor of such a choice is sufficient to prove this. The authority of the older theologians is not to be invoked in this matter. The question which was proposed by the older theologians is not the same as that problem with which we are now concerned. Moral theologians said that it was not licit to use at the same time a double probability for the non-existence of a double precept when it is certain that by using both probabilities, one of the precepts must of necessity be violated. This is substantially a case proposed by De Lugo: in the night intervening between the vigil of Pentecost and the day of Pentecost itself, Titus, on account of the differences of time registered by different clocks, says that there is a probability that the feast of Pentecost had already been reached. Can

282 Michiels, *Normae Generales Iuris Canonici*, II, 148; Van Hove, *De Consuetudine, de Temporis Supputatione*, p. 262; Vermeersch, *Theologia Moralis*, I, 352.

283 Michiels, *loc. cit.*; Ferland, "L'Avance de l'Heure et Certains Préceptes de l' Eglise," *Semaine Religieuse de Québec*, XXXV (1923), 296.

he eat meat as if it were the day of Pentecost itself, and arguing that probably Pentecost has not yet arrived, go to Communion on the feast itself?

De Lugo gives this solution: Titus could not eat meat unless it was already the feast itself, in which event he could not go to Communion, since he would have broken his Eucharistic fast. Therefore, he had no right to feel safe in eating meat and then going to Communion under the circumstances as set forth in the case.[284]

The case which De Lugo gives is that of two clocks which showed different times. One indicated that it was already past midnight, and the other that it was not yet midnight. In the solution of the case the rules of probabilism were applied. It was not a case of a formal concession or right, such as is granted by canon 33, of choosing any of the various computable times in the fulfillment of certain ecclesiastical precepts. They are altogether different matters, and the principles of solution that are applied in the one case need not necessarily be employed in the solution of the other.[285]

According to canon 18, ecclesiastical laws are to be understood according to the proper meaning of the words in the text and the context. The contents of canon 33 in their obvious and proper sense imply that one may indifferently adopt one or any of the variously computable times. It does not say that when one has chosen one kind of time, he must necessarily follow the same kind of time for all the remaining precepts.[286]

Woywod says: "If the priest eats meat on the assumption that Saturday has begun after midnight daylight saving time, it seems correct to declare that he cannot say Mass on

[284] "Debet sequi unum et idem horologium pro utroque praecepto."—*De Sacramento Eucharistiae*, disp. XV, sect. 2, n. 53.

[285] Vermeersch, *Theologia Moralis*, I, 351; Michiels, *Normae Generales Iuris Canonici*, II, 143.

[286] Ferland, "L'Avance de l'Heure et Certains Préceptes de l'Eglise," *Semaine Religieuse de Québec*, XXXV (1923), 616-617.

Saturday. In connection with the same action or obligation, it would appear utterly inconsistent to consider the same period of time as part of both Friday and Saturday."[287] However, in an article in the *Homiletic Monthly and Pastoral Review* he says that upon reconsidering the matter he would not insist that it is unreasonable to make use of two different computations of time, for instance to employ daylight saving time in relation to the Friday abstinence, but standard time in relation to the Eucharistic fast, so that a priest who has eaten between twelve and one o'clock A.M. daylight saving time on Saturday might nevertheless say Mass on the following morning.[288]

Since the hour of midnight is to be reckoned physically, it must be determined whether midnight is indicated by the first or the last stroke of the clock. In other words, may one go to Holy Communion when he has eaten after the first stroke of twelve o'clock but before the last stroke of the clock? It is more commonly held that midnight is indicated by the first stroke of the clock, and consequently that the law of the Eucharistic fast binds from the time that the clock begins to strike twelve.[289] There are, however, some authors who think otherwise. For instance, the Salmanticenses say that the hour of midnight is completed only at the last stroke of the clock, because the twelve strokes of the clock are morally computed as one.[290]

Though the opinion which holds that the first striking of the clock designates the hour of midnight is the more prob-

[287] *A Practical Commentary on the Code of Canon Law*, I, 19.

[288] Woywod, "Daylight Saving Time and the Obligations in Which the Point of Time Is Important," *Homiletic Monthly and Pastoral Review*, 2 series, XXXVII (1937), 963.

[289] Thomas Sanchez, *De Sancto Matrimonii Sacramento* (3 vols., Lugduni: 1739), lib. II, disp. XLI, n. 40; S. Alphonsus, *Theologia Moralis*, VI, 282; De Lugo, *De Sacramento Eucharistiae*, disp. XV, sect, 2, n. 38; Concina, *Theologia Christiana* (10 vols., Romae: 1749-1751), tom. V, lib. II, diss. 3, cap. 18, n. 5; Bucceroni, *Theologia Moralis* (3 ed., 2 vols., Romae: 1898), II, 181.

[290] Salmanticenses, *Cursus Theologiae Moralis* (6 vols., Venetiis: 1728), tom. I, tract. 4, cap. 7, n. 63.

able one, yet the contrary opinion enjoys a certain amount of probability, and may be followed in practice, since it is not certain that all the clocks are so accurately timed that they indicate the hour of midnight at the first stroke of twelve.[291]

Only when one is certain of having broken the Eucharistic fast is he obliged to abstain from going to Holy Communion. The reason is that a doubtful law does not oblige. The breaking of the Eucharistic fast is a fact which must be proved, or which at least must be certain, before it can be said that one is obliged to abstain from receiving Holy Communion because he has broken his fast. For the case of a positive doubt, namely, when one has serious reasons for believing that he might have broken the natural fast, this same doctrine is supported by at least a probable opinion and may therefore be followed in practice.[292] While the doubt remains the obligation of abstaining from the reception of Holy Communion cannot be urged.

Formerly theologians were not agreed whether it was lawful or unlawful for a person to receive Holy Communion where there existed a well-founded doubt that the person had observed the fast required for Holy Communion. The one opinion held that under no circumstances was it licit to receive Holy Communion unless one was certain that he has kept the fast prescribed from the midnight preceding the reception of Holy Communion. No one, they argued can receive Holy Communion unless he knows himself to be worthy. Therefore, let him prove himself worthy, or else abstain.[293]

On the other hand the Probabilists maintained that one might licitly go to Holy Communion if he had probable reasons to believe that he did not eat or drink after midnight.

[291] Cappello, *Tractatus Canonico-Moralis de Sacramentis*, I, 462.

[292] Cappello, *Tractatus Canonico-Moralis de Sacramentis*, I, 463; Bucceroni, *Theologia Moralis*, II, 180.

[293] Thomas Sanchez, *De Sancto Matrimonii Sacramento*, lib. II, disp. XLI, n. 40; Concina, *Theologia Christiana*, tom. VIII, lib. III, diss. 1, cap. 3, n. 4; Salmanticenses, *Cursus Theologiae Moralis*, tom. I, tract. 4, cap. 7, n. 69.

Such a probable reason would obtain, for instance, if one was accustomed always to note the time of midnight, and judged that the hour of midnight had not struck. The Probabilists based their opinion on the principle: *Melior est conditio possidentis.* However, they did not agree in the application of this principle. Some maintained that it was lawful to receive Holy Communion when you were sure of the fact that you had partaken of food or drink and doubted only concerning the time, namely, whether it was before or after midnight that you partook of the same, or also when you were sure that you were fasting at midnight and doubted merely whether or not you ate anything after that time. Others made a distinction between the two cases of doubt, and held that in case you were sure that you were fasting at midnight and doubted only whether afterwards you broke the fast, you could receive Holy Communion, whereas, if you were sure that you ate or drank something around midnight, but were not sure whether it was before or after midnight, it was not lawful to receive Holy Communion.[294]

Present day theologians discard all distinctions and maintain that in any case of doubt about the fact whether one has partaken of food or drink, and whether or not it was after midnight, one may receive Holy Communion.[295]

When two or more clocks vary in time, it is permissible to follow the one which strikes last, provided that the clock we choose to follow is one which ordinarily keeps good time, and provided that there be not present any direct or evident indication of its possible and probable errancy.[296] Two

[294] Layman, *Theologia Moralis*, Vol. I, lib. I, tract. 4, cap. 6, n. 36; Cf. De Lugo, *De Sacramento Eucharistiae*, disp. XV, sect. 2, n. 41-45.

[295] Gasparri, *De Eucharistia*, I, 305; Noldin, *Theologia Moralis*, III, 169; Bucceroni, *Theologia Moralis*, II, 180; Vermeersch, *Theologia Moralis*, I, 345; Cappello, *Tractatus Canonico-Moralis de Sacramentis*, I, 463; Tummulo-Jorio, II, 215.

[296] Thomas Sanchez, *De Sancto Matrimonii Sacramente*, lib. II, disp. XLI, n. 40; S. Alphonsus, *Theologia Moralis*, VI, 282; Gasparri, *De Eucharistia*, I, 305; Cicognani, Canon Law, p. 684; "Cas de Conscience," *Analecta Iuris Pontificii*, XIII (1874), 606-607.

clocks indicating different times, are like two probable opinions. We may choose between them. However, one may not choose to follow both at the same time. Hence, if one elects to follow the time indicated by one of these clocks for one obligation, he must follow the same clock in the fulfillment of all obligations which are to be fulfilled simultaneously or consecutively.[297]

In the use of a choice of the variously computed times, as granted by the Code in canon 33, a fact to be noted and never to be overlooked is that the obligation of the natural fast is an extremely definite one. It begins to bind at the very moment of midnight. It does not begin to bind before midnight for ever so short a space of time. Once midnight is passed by any interval of time, no matter how diminutive this interval may be, it asserts its full binding power. Indeed the hour of midnight is to be reckoned in accord with standards of physical accuracy, and not only according to the demands of a moral approximation. Hence, due care must always be taken, lest the liberty which the code grants relative to a choice of computable times become an occasion which would betray one into using a very wide, or even lax, interpretation of what the Code denotes by the phrase *media nox*.[298]

[297] Concina, *Theologia Christiana*, tom. V, lib. II, diss. 2, cap. 18, n. 5.

[298] The positive law does not prescribe a fast after the reception of Holy Communion. However, a certain demand of natural reverence for the Blessed Sacrament prompts us to abstain from eating or drinking anything immediately after receiving Holy Communion. Saint Thomas says that there should be some time intervening between the reception of Holy Communion and the act of eating or drinking. cf. *Summa Theologia*, pars. III, q. LXXX, a. 8, ad 6. Saint Alphonsus held that one should wait for fifteen mainutes before eating or drinking after receiving Holy Communion. Cf. *Theologia Moralis*, VI, 283. Hence, as a practice or rule of action it is not licit to eat or drink immediately after the reception of Communion. Nevertheless, in a case of necessity or for a just cause one may do so provided that by so doing there is no irreverence shown to the Blessed Sacrament. Cf. Cappello, *Tractatus Canonico-Moralis de Sacramentis*, I, 480; S. Alphonsus, *Theologia Moralis*, VI, 283; "Cas de Conscience," *Analecta Iuris Pontificii*, XIII (1874), 607-608.

CHAPTER III

CAUSES EXCUSING FROM THE EUCHARISTIC FAST

The reasons which are deemed valid to excuse one from the obligation of the Eucharistic fast can be divided into two categories, namely the exceptions which are stated in the common law, and by way of supplement, the exceptional circumstances of particular cases in which canonists commonly teach that it would be permitted for one to forego the ecclesiastical law of the fast in favor of a higher law or a more urgent obligation. These cases of extraordinary circumstances imply an extension of the exceptions incorporated in the law.

The cases in which one is excused by the law itself from observing the Eucharistic fast before the reception of Holy Communion are: when one is in danger of death;[299] in a limited manner, and under certain conditions, when a sick person has been confined to bed for a month;[300] when necessity arises to prevent irreverence to the Blessed Sacrament;[301] and finally when a catechumen in the observance of the rubrics prescribed by the Ritual is given a pinch of blessed salt during the ceremonial rite that precedes his baptism.[302] Because of the specific importance of the question of the Communion of the sick and the correspondingly longer treatment the discussion of the question will not be undertaken here in its place, but left for another chapter expressly devoted to it.

The Church, ever mindful of the words of Christ, "un-

299 Canon 858, ¶ 1.
300 Canon 858, ¶ 2.
301 Canon 858, ¶ 1.
302 *Rituale Romanum*, tit. II, c. *Ordo baptismi adultorum*, n. 15.

less you eat the flesh of the Son of Man and drink His blood, you shall not have life in you,"[303] and aware of the extreme importance that those who are about to enter into eternity should be refreshed for this arduous journey, has made every possible concession that they might receive the Holy Eucharist in the form of Viaticum. Thus, from the very earliest ages there has been always an exception made in the canons relating to the Eucharistic fast for those who were in danger of death.[304] Nor has there ever been any question concerning this among theologians.

In danger of death, from whatever cause it may proceed, the faithful are bound by precept to receive Holy Communion.[305] Whether this precept is divine or ecclesiastical is not certain. Most authors say that it is divine or at least a divine ecclesiastical law.

The Archbishop of Cincinnati asked when penitents could be said to be in danger (*in periculo*) or at the point (*in articulo*) of death. The Holy Office referred him to approved authors.[306]

This question was asked with reference to the eventual absolution from all censures and sins no matter how reserved. Nevertheless, the interpretation of what is meant

[303] John, VI, 54.

[304] Martinus V ([in Conc. Constantien.], const. *"In eminentis,"* 22 febr. 1418): ". . .*sacrorum Canonum auctoritas laudabilis, et approbata consuetudo ecclesiae servavit et servat, quod, huiusmodi sacramentum non debet. . .a fidelibus recipi non ieiunis, nisi, in infirmitatis, aut alterus necessitatis, a iure vel ecclesia concesso, vel admisso,"*—*Fontes*, n. 44. I Council of Nice (325) c. 13—Schroeder, *Disciplinary Decrees of the General Councils*, p. 42: Canon 13 of the I Council of Nice insists on the administration of Holy Viaticum to the dying, even to those who as *lapsi* had not yet fulfilled their term of penance. It does not say anything to the effect that fasting is not required. The Council's insistence however, that Holy Viaticum be given to the dying might very well imply that, for it states without condition: "If anyone be near death let him not be deprived of the last and most necessary Viaticum."; cf. also, *Decretum Burchardi*, lib. V. c. 35—MPL, CXL, 759; Lamy, *Resolutiones Canonicae Timothei Alexandrini—De Syrorum Fide et Disciplina*, p. 183.

[305] Canon 864, ¶ 1.

[306] S. C. S. Off. (Cincinnat.), 13 sept. 1859—*Fontes*, n. 955.

by *periculum mortis* or by *articulus mortis* remains the same in relation to the administration of Holy Viaticum.

Danger of death (*periculum mortis*) is not the same thing as the moment of death (*articulus mortis*). Danger of death means that the person is in such a state that he has equal chances for life or death. In other words, it means that condition of circumstances in which a person is placed when it is truly and gravely probable that he may live or that he may die. Therefore, when the expected early approach of a person's death is probable, that is, even though it is neither imminent nor as yet morally certain, one may rightly consider that person to be in danger of death.[307] In law, danger of death and the moment of death are taken in the same sense.

The danger of death must be reckoned morally. In case of prudent doubt about the previous chance to live the priest may proceed to administer Holy Viaticum to a sick person who is not fasting, provided of course, that there is no obvious danger of irreverence.[308]

Danger of death may arise either from an intrinsic or from an extrinsic cause, v.g., from sickness, from a wound, from a difficult child-birth, from a surgical operation, from extreme old age, from war, from pestilence, or from a perilous journey. Since canon 864, ¶1, obliges the faithful to receive the Holy Eucharist when they are in danger of death, be it from any cause whatsoever, and since canon 858, ¶1, states that the Eucharistic fast does not oblige those who receive the Holy Eucharist when they are in danger of death, it should make no difference whether the danger arises from an intrinsic or from an extrinsic cause. Some moralists and canonists however make a distinction in re-

[307] Cappello, *Tractatus Canonico-Moralis de Sacramentis*, I, 438-439; D'Annibale, *Summula Theologiae Moralis* (5 ed., 3 vol., Romae: 1908), I, 38; cf. also, S. Alphonsus, *Theologia Moralis*, VI, 561.

[308] S. Alphonsus, *Theologia Moralis*, VI, 289; Cappello, *Tractatus Canonico-Moralis de Sacramentis*, I, 484; Vermeersch-Creusen, *Epitome Iuris Canonici*, II, 85.

gard to this point between those who are constituted in danger of death from an intrinsic or from an extrinsic cause.[309] According to a strict interpretation of the law and from a response of the Sacred Congregation of the Propagation of the Faith this distinction appears to be unwarranted.[310] While this response does not explicitly declare that those who are condemned to death are excused from the Eucharistic fast if they receive the Holy Eucharist on the day of their execution, or on the day previous, yet this seems implied from the fact that the Holy Eucharist was to be administered to them in the form of Viaticum. Canon 858, ¶1, makes no mention of the fact whether danger of death proceeds from an intrinsic or from an extrinsic cause. Where the law does not distinguish, no distinction should be made.[311]

Prümmer does not allow even those who are in danger of death from sickness to receive Viaticum while not fasting, if they are able to observe the Eucharistic fast with reasonable ease.[312] Vermeersch-Creusen, while admitting that not only the sick but also those who are in danger of death from an extrinsic cause are excused by the law, nevertheless say that in the latter case it is necessary that they cannot conveniently wait until another day when they are fasting, whereas the sick have a strict right to receive Viaticum without observing the fast, even apart from the presence of any other reason.[313] Apparently, the reason for

309 Augustine, *A Commentary on the New Code of Canon Law,* IV, 234; Noldin, *De Sacramentis,* III, 174.

310 S. C. de Prop. Fide (C. P. pro Sin. Tunkin. Occident. 21 iul 1841): "*Quid, de christianis vel sacerdotibus propter fidem no solum ad carceres perpetuos vel temporales damnatis, sed ad mortem laqueo vel gladio subeundam? Potestne illis deferri Sanctissimum Sacramentum pridie, vel ipso die eorum executionis? Et tunc debet illis administrari tamquam Viaticum moribundis, vel tamquam communio ordinaria benevalentibus? Resp. Affirmative, et per modum Viatici.*"—*Fontes,* n. 4789.

311 Woywod, *A Practical Commentary on the Code of Canon Law,* I, 416; Many, *Praelectiones de Missa cum Appendice de Sanctissimo Sacramento Eucharistiae,* p. 340.

312 *Theologia Moralis,* III, 152.

313 *Epitome Iuris Canonici,* II, 85.

this distinction is that ordinarily those who are in danger of death from sickness find it morally impossible to keep the natural fast. While this distinction has a foundation in fact, it has none in law. It is true that in the case of one who is in possible danger of death from an extrinsic cause, there might be more occasion for abuse, but it can be left to the prudent judgment of the priest to prevent such abuses. In a particular case he would be perfectly justified in refusing Viaticum to a prospective communicant when he is not fasting if there existed a well grounded fear of consequent irreverence or scandal.[314]

Previous to the promulgation of the Code there was a dispute as to how often one could receive Viaticum in the same sickness. Saint Alphonsus held that seven or eight days should intervene between the two receptions.[315] Suarez insisted on eight or ten days.[316] This was the more common view and was considered the more probable opinion. However, Benedict XIV and not a few others were of the opinion that Holy Communion might be administered in the form of Viaticum many times, and that there was no necessity for such a long interval between the repeated administrations.[317] Layman says that for a just cause, v.g., if one was accustomed to receive Communion often out of devotion, a person might be permitted to receive Holy Viaticum every other day.[318]

That Holy Viaticum may be administered many times in the same sickness is now certain from canon 864, ¶3: "While the danger of death lasts, Holy Viaticum lawfully may and becomingly ought to be administered in accordance with the prudent counsel of the confessor repeatedly on separate days." Since the canon merely says that Viati-

[314] Coucke, "De Ieiunio Eucharistico," *Collationes Brugensis*, XXXIV (1934), 383.

[315] *Theologia Moralis*, VI, 284.

[316] *De Sacramento Eucharistiae*, disp. LXVIII, sect. 5.

[317] *De Synodo Dioecesana*, lib. VI, cap. 12.

[318] *Theologia Moralis*, I, lib. V, tract. IV, cap. 6, n. 20.

cum may be administered many times and does not limit the administration to any certain number of times, there is no reason why a person in danger of death could not receive Holy Viaticum daily.[319]

A patient about to undergo a serious operation may be considered in danger of death and hence, be excused from the law of the Eucharistic fast in order to receive Holy Viaticum. Because of the progress of medical science in late years many operations which formerly were considered major ones are now classed as minor, since there seems to be little danger to life. While this is true, yet experience has taught that a considerable number of persons are still taken by death after a serious abdominal operation, and this seems to be sufficient reason for saying that persons who face a serious operation may be considered as being in danger of death before such operations. Consequently, if a priest is willing to act on this explanation there is no reason why he cannot administer Holy Communion in the form of Viaticum in such a case to a person who is not fasting, provided the operation is a serious one and that it is to be the person's last Communion before the operation. Moralists teach that a person about to undergo a serious operation is bound to receive Holy Viaticum. Hence, Holy Communion could be administered as Viaticum to a person just before undergoing a serious operation, even though he had broken his fast.[320] Nor is it necessary that one should scrupulously inquire into whether it be certain that there is serious danger to life, since moral certainty is not required. Yet, neither would the mere possibility of death which always exists, nor a slight or minimal probability of ensuing death, be sufficient. What is required and suffices is that there is a reasonable probability that the

[319] Cappello, *Tractatus Canonico-Moralis de Sacramentis*, I, 442.

[320] Coucke, "De Ieiunio Eucharistico," *Collationes Brugensis*, XXXIV (1934), 383; Woywod, "Answers to Questions," *Homiletic Monthly and Pastoral Review*, 1 series, XXXIII (1932), 638; Twomey, "The Eucharistic Fast," *ER*, CII (1940), 416.

danger of death exists. In case of doubt about the actual danger, Viaticum may and should be administered to those who are not fasting.[321]

Another practical question may arise with regard to the observance of the Eucharistic fast for the reception of Holy Communion on the part of soldiers before they proceed to the front. A response of the Sacred Penitentiary, March 18, 1912, and May 29, 1915, declared that every soldier who is in a state of warlike assembly, or of "mobilization", can *ipso facto* be considered as in danger of death, so that he can be absolved by any priest he meets.[322] Though this response was given in answer to a particular question in a special crisis and was formulated especially in regard to sacramental absolution, yet it can serve with regard to all soldiers similarly situated to manifest the application of a like principle of action to reach a similar solution. The principle underlying this particular response also lends itself, *servatis servandis,* to utilization and adaptation in the question dealing with the reception of Holy Viaticum.

The doubt, which was proposed by Monsignor Cholly, Bishop of Verdun, inquired, "whether any soldier who has been called to arms, or, as it is expressed, *mobilized,* is by that very fact placed in danger of death, so that he may be absolved by any priest he meets". The Sacred Penitentiary changed the wording of the doubt to read: "Whether every soldier who has been called to arms, or *mobilized,* can by that very fact be placed on the same footing with those who are in danger of death, so that he may be absolved by any priest he meets". The reply was: "In the affirmative, according to the accepted rules laid down by

321 Litt. Ap., "*Sodalitatem,*" May 31, 1921: "Qui in discrimine ultimo versantur, sacri viatici et extremae Untionis susceptionem ne eo usque remorentur cum sensum amissuri iam sunt, sed, contra, quemadmodum Ecclesia docet et praecipit, iis roborentur Sacramentis vixdum, ingravascente morbo, prudens fiat de periculo mortis iudicium—*AAS*, XIII, 342; Twomey, *loc. cit.*

322 *AAS*, VII (1915), 282.

authors." That those who are mobilized may be absolved by any priest they approach for sacramental absolution is clear from the wording of the declaration. The tenor of the "doubt" in its changed formulation manifests that the answer was a concession on the part of the Sacred Penitentiary.[323]

Relative to this decree there is a doubt proposed by the Cardinal Archbishop of Lyons on November 25, 1914. The doubt was proposed to the Sacred Congregation of the Holy Office under this formula: "Whether soldiers *in procinctu*, or, as they say, mobilized for war, ought to be considered as constituted in the near danger of death so that Holy Communion may be administered to them while not fasting." The answer was given December 10, 1914, and was in the negative.[324]

Another decree issued by the Sacred Congregation for the Discipline of the Sacraments on February 11, 1915, declared that "soldiers who are called to battle may be admitted *servatis servandis* to the reception of the Holy Eucharist after the manner of Viaticum."[325]

The application of the principle stated in these decrees and responses presents some difficulty. Do the words, "*Milites ad proelium vocatos,*" mean only those soldiers who are at the front? The Italian phrase, "*I soldati sul fronte,*" appear to suggest that they do, but if such were the case it does not seem that a special decree would have been needed in their favor. For those in the front lines there is evidently a very probable danger of death, and consequently they *ipso facto* come under the general provision made by the Church for those in danger of death. It is not question

323 O'Donnell, "Administration of the Viaticum to Soldiers Ordered to the Front," *IER*, 5 series, VI (1915), 626.

324 *Le Canoniste Contemporain*, XXXVIII (1915), 455.

325 S. C. S., *decr.* 11 febr. 1915: "Milites ad proelium vocatos (i soldati sul fronte) admitti posse servatis servandis ad S. Mensam Eucharisticam per modum Viatici."—*AAS*, VII (1915), 97; *Cf.* also, *Le Canoniste Contemporain*, XXXVIII (1915), 73-75.

here of those in the front lines. The discussion was concerned rather with those who were mobilized and under orders to proceed to some unknown front. While they were not actually in danger, and might not be for some time to come, there was always the probability of a proximate engagement for them before they would have had a chance to receive Holy Viaticum. Hence, if there was a probability that they might be called into action, they could be allowed to receive Holy Communion in the form of Viaticum even though they were not fasting, provided it was reasonably probable that this was to be their last opportunity for receiving Holy Communion. Then the next day, they can receive Holy Viaticum again for the same reason; and so *daily* as long as the threat of combat remains.[326]

The dispensation from the Eucharistic fast was not granted to all soldiers by the very fact that they were in the army, but was restricted to those who were in actual danger, or who would in all probability be subject to actual danger before they would have an opportunity to receive Holy Communion in the ordinary manner and while not fasting. It obtained only in such cases where the conditions contemplated by the Sacred Congregation of the Sacraments in its decree were fully verified. Hence, those who were not in these circumstances, *v.g.*, those who were mobilized but not under orders to proceed to any front, could not be made the beneficiaries of the concession of receiving Holy Communion while not fasting. The circumstances in which these soldiers who were merely mobilized were such that they quite readily made feasible for them the reception of Holy Communion while fasting.[327]

Since the reception of Viaticum is not limited to one time only, but is allowed to be administered repeatedly on distinct days as often as the situation of the soldiers war-

[326] O'Donnell, "Administration of the Viaticum to Soldiers Ordered to the Front," *IER*, 5 series, VI (1915).

[327] Boudinhon, "A propos des Aumôniers Militaires et Prêtres Soldats," *Le Canoniste Contemporain*, XXXIX (1916), 38.

ranted it, they could receive every day *per modum viatici,* and consequently even though they were not fasting. There was nothing in the text of the decree which warranted a restriction of the reception of Holy Viaticum to one time only. As often as the soldiers were at the front or were under orders to proceed to the front within a short time, they could receive without fasting.[328]

This same right would also be available for the crews of submarines and other warships when on active duty in the combat area, and to the crews of merchant-men whose courses are charted through submarine or mine-infested waters, provided that the danger is such that they could not await the following day to receive while fasting.[329]

The second exception to the law of the Eucharistic fast contained in canon 858, ¶1, is had when it becomes necessary to consume the Blessed Sacrament to safeguard it from irreverence. Such a necessity would exist, v.g., if a church were on fire or about to be destroyed or desecrated by invading hordes or mobs, leaving no time to remove the Blessed Sacrament to a safe place. In these and like cases a priest, or even a lay person, if there were no priest present, not only could but should consume the consecrated host, even though he was not fasting. The law of fasting before Communion, which was made to insure a due reverence for the Holy Eucharist, ceases to bind when by its observance in such extraordinary cases the Blessed Sacrament could certainly be subjected to an irreverence.[330]

Finally, the Roman Ritual, treating of the baptism of adults, indicates another case in which one who is not fasting is allowed to receive Holy Communion. The Ritual prescribes that a pinch of blessed salt be placed in the mouth of the catechumen. In accordance with the pre-

[328] Boudinhon, *op. cit.,* 37; cf. *Le Canoniste Contemporain,* XXXVIII (1915), 74.
[329] Twomey, "The Eucharistic Fast," *ER,* CII (1940), 416.
[330] S. Alphonsus, *Theologia Moralis,* VI, n. 287.

scriptions of the Ritual, the ceremony of Baptism having been completed, Mass is then celebrated, if it is at a suitable hour, and the newly baptized are to assist at the Mass and receive Holy Communion.[331] The salt which is given to a newly baptized convert certainly does break the Eucharistic fast. However, the Church, when she made these liturgical laws, tacitly, insofar as it is necessary, dispensed from the law of the Eucharistic fast.[332]

Further exceptions to the law of the Eucharistic fast, relative to the priest and the celebration of Mass are contained in the Rubrics of the Roman Missal, edited by Pius V, in 1570. These exceptions pertain to: 1) the completion of the Holy Sacrifice of the Mass; 2) the case in which invalid matter is used for the Sacrifice; and 3) the consumption of the particles of the Sacred Holy after the Communion of the Mass.

The first exception, that of completing the Holy Sacrifice of the Mass was mentioned in the VII Council of Toledo. The canon of this Council was later incorporated in the Decree of Gratian.[333] If after the Consecration of one or both of the Sacred Species the celebrant is suddenly stricken or becomes gravely ill, so that he cannot finish the Mass, then another priest, and in case of necessity even when he is not fasting, should continue with the Mass and complete the Holy Sacrifice. The Divine Law that the Sacrifice should not be left incomplete takes precedence over the ecclesiastical law of the Eucharistic fast. If a sudden sickness overtakes the celebrating priest before the consecration of either Species, it is not necessary that the Mass be completed, for the Sacrifice begins only with the consecration of one of the Species.[334] It is worthy of note that a

331 *Rituale Romanum*, tit. II, c. 4, *Ordo baptismi adultorum*, n. 15.

332 S. C. de Prop. Fide, *instr.* (ad Vic. ap. Tunk, Orient.), 16 febr. 1806—*Collectanea S. Congregationis de Propaganda Fide*, n. 687.

333 VII Council of Toledo, c. 2—Manis, X, 767; c. 16, C. VII, q. 1.

334 *Missale Romanum* (tit. *De defectibus in celebratione missarum occurentibus*, c. X, *De defectibus in ministerio ipso occurrentibus*, n. 3): Si post consecrationem Corporis tantum, ante consecrationem

priest who is called upon to finish a Mass in this case cannot say another Mass on the same day unless he has the faculty of binating.[335] A priest who has already begun Mass and who then recalls that he is not fasting may proceed with the Mass if he becomes aware of that fact only after the consecration of either Species. The reason is the same as that given above, namely, the divine law demands that the Holy Sacrifice once begun should be completed. If the priest realizes that he has broken his fast before the consecration of either Species he should leave the altar if he thinks he could prudently do so without giving occasion for scandal. If the Mass is celebrated in a public place with the faithful assisting, then the danger of scandal would almost always be present, since the people might not understand how the priest could have broken his fast or how it was possible that the priest did not remember that he had done so.[336]

The Rubrics of the Missal also prescribe that when a priest has arrived at the Communion of the Mass and only then adverts to the fact that the bread or wine used by him was not valid matter for the Sacrifice, he is to take new valid matter, make the sacrificial offering of it, and begin with the words *Qui pridie quam pateretur* for its consecration, even in the event that he has broken his fast through the previous consumption of the matter used. If the Mass is publicly attended, then for the sake of avoiding any likely scandal the Rubrics allow the priest to make the sacrificial offering, to consecrate the matter and then immediately to consume the Consecrated Species.[337] In case the invalid matter happens to be the bread it is required that the priest

Sanguinis, vel utroque, consecrato, id accidit, Sacerdos graviter infirmatur, Missa per alium sacerdotem expleatur ab eo loco ubi ille desiit, et in casu necessitatis *etiam per non ieiunum*.

[335] S. R. C., 16 dec. 1823—*Decr. Auth.*, n. 2630.

[336] S. Thomas, *Summa*, Pars III, q. LXXXIII, a. 6; Prümmer, *Theologia Moralis*, III, 151; Noldin, *Theologia Moralis*, III, 172; Cappello, *Tractatus Canonico-Moralis de Sacramentis*, I, 482.

[337] *Missale Romanum*, tit. *De defectibus in celebratione missarum occurrentibus*, c. III, *de defectu panis*, nn. 5, 6.

procure only a new host. However, should the priest have already consumed the Sacred Host before he discovers that the wine was not valid matter, it is necessary for him to take a new host and new wine which is valid matter and again consecrate both substances.[338]

Finally, one more case may arise in which it is permitted for the priest to consume the consecrated Species after having broken his fast, namely, when the celebrant upon taking the ablutions discovers that there are particles or fragments of the Sacred Species remaining on the corporal.[339] The reason given by the Rubrics is that these particles are part of the same Sacrifice, and hence, may be consumed, even after the celebrant has alrady taken the ablutions. If there be question of an integral host, whether large or small, the priest may not consume it after having taken the ablutions unless he must do so to guard it from irreverence, *v.g.*, if there is not at hand a tabernacle or some other honorable and decorous place for the preservation of the consecrated Host until the next Mass is offered.[340]

If at Mass the particle of the consecrated Host adheres to the lip of the Chalice, the Rubrics also give the priest the choice of removing it with his finger or of pouring a little wine into the chalice to remove it.[341]

Likewise in accordance with the liturgy on Good Friday a particle of the consecrated Host is placed in unconsecrated wine and the two are consumed together. Even though part of the Sacred Host remains after the wine has been swal-

338 *Missale Romanum*, tit. *De defectibus in celebratione missarum occurrentibus*, c. III, *De defectu panis*, nn. 5, 6, c. IV, *De defectu vini*, n. 5.

339 *Missale Romanum*, tit. *De defectibus in celebratione missarum occurrentibus*, c. VII, *De defectu intentionis*, nn. 2, 3.

340 *Missale Romanum*, *loc. cit.;* cf. Saint Alphonsus, *Theologia Moralis*, VI, 251; Many, *Praelectiones de Missa cum Appendice de Sanctissimo Sacramento Eucharistiae*, p. 338; *Clergy Review*, XVI (1939), 356.

341 *Missale Romanum*, tit. *De defectibus in celebratione missarum occurrentibus*, c. X, *De defectibus in Ministerio ipso occurrentibus*, n. 10.

lowed, one need not scruple that he has broken his fast.[342]

Besides these exceptions which are contained explicitly in the law, there are some other exceptional circumstances in which canonists would allow the law of the Eucharistic fast to be foregone in favor of a more pressing obligation. These cases may be reduced to the following: 1) the danger of grave scandal or infamy, 2) the avoidance of grave inconvenience, 3) the necessity of administering Viaticum to the dying, and, 4) the necessity of fulfilling the Paschal precept when one is unable to keep the fast.

In connection with the excusing cause of the danger of scandal there immediately arises the question whether or not a priest may say a second Mass for the people on a Sunday or Holyday of Obligation; if through inadvertence he has broken his fast by taking the ablutions in the first Mass.

A Council held at Nismes in 1284 decreed: "If not all the parishioners are able to assist at one Mass because they live at different places which are far distant from the Church, as in the mountains, and there are not two priests resident at the Church, then the one priest who has already offered a Mass may nevertheless offer up a second Mass upon the request of the parishioners who have just arrived. However, a priest may not offer a second Mass when he has taken the ablutions in the Mass already offered by him."[343]

Benedict XIV cites this canon of the Council of Nismes in his letter, "*Declarasti*". His doctrine on the subject is no less explicit.[344] A decision of the Holy office given in 1874 in answer to a proposed doubt replied that fear of scandal or wonderment on the part of the people would not justify a priest in saying a second Mass if he had broken his fast.[345]

342 *Missale Romanum, Feria VI in Parasceve.*
343 *De Celebratione Missarum*—Mansi, XXIV, 538-539.
344 Benedictus XIV, ep. "*Declarasti,*" 176 mart. 1746—*Fontes*, n. 265.
345 S. C. S. Off. (*Vallisprat*), 2 dec. 1874—Fontes, n. 1034.

This answer does not seem to deal with this question as one of legal principle. In other words it does not imply that the observance of the ecclesiastical law of the Eucharistic fast for the celebration of Mass is a law of a higher order than is the divine law which calls upon men to avoid scandal. The answer is rather concerned with a disputable question of fact, that apparently was assumed in the proposed query. The query assumes that the saying of a second Mass by a priest who is no longer fasting might be justified on the score that scandal can in no other way be avoided. Hence, the interpretation of this decision of the Holy Office is that for reasons of scandal and wonderment the second Mass may not be said, simply because with a reasonable effort all scandal and wonderment can be forestalled, when the law of the Church is properly explained to the people. A changed view point concerning this question of fact has emerged since 1874. In the opinion of the majority of present day theologians and canonists, this danger of scandal is nearly always present in such a case. Hence, they would allow a priest to say a second Mass in these circumstances.[346]

All theologians are agreed that the fact alone, that the faithful would be deprived of Mass on a Sunday or a day of Obligation would not be sufficient cause to allow a priest to say Mass if he had broken his fast.[347] The reason that they give is that the law of the Eucharistic fast is more serious than that of the precept obliging the faithful to hear Mass on Sundays. Hence, it can be concluded that if the question is considered absolutely without any com-

[346] Many, *Praelectiones de Missa cum Appendice de Sanctissimo Sanctissimo Eucharistiae*, p. 344; Noldin, *Theologia Moralis*, III, 173; Cappello, *Tractatus Canonico-Moralis de Sacramentis*, I, 482; Prümmer, *Theologia Moralis*, III, 152; Vermeersch, *Theologia Moralis*, III, 316; Genicot, *Casus Conscientiae*, II, 225.
225.

[347] S. Alphonsus, *Theologia Moralis*, VI, 287; Suarez, *De Sacramento Eucharistiae*, disp. LXVIII, sect. 5, n. 5; De Lugo, *De Sacramento Eucharistiae*, disp. XV, sect. 2, n. 68; cf. the authors mentioned in the previous footnote.

plication of danger of scandal or loss of reputation, the law of the Eucharistic fast must be regarded as the more urgent of the two precepts, and the sole reason that the faithful would otherwise not be able to fulfill their Sunday obligation is not sufficient to excuse from the law obliging the priest to be fasting for Mass.

However, theologians are equally agreed that if there is danger of scandal the priest would be justified in saying his second Mass regardless of the fact that he had broken his fast.[348] Not all are agreed that there is present a danger of scandal or infamy in a case in which a priest who has to binate, unintentionally takes the ablutions in his first Mass. Those who say that no such danger is present argue that the priest could easily and prudently inform the people that he could not say a second Mass because he had inadvertently taken the ablutions in his first Mass.[349] However, the majority of authors grant that in practice this question cannot be considered apart from the circumstances of scandal or loss of reputation.[350]

It might be objected that the reply of the Holy Office excludes scandal as a justifying cause. As we remarked this reply of the Holy Office was considering the question as a matter of fact, and not as a principle of law. While it may have been as true a hundred years ago, that the faithful would not take any offense or scandal from the fact that a priest could not say Mass because he had broken his fast, it seems that at the present time, with the changed conditions of people and times, there would be danger of scandal if the priest had to tell the assembled congregation that he had broken his fast, and could not say Mass. There would be a lurking suspicion in the minds of at least some of the

[348] *Cf. supra*, footnote 346.

[349] Gasparri, *De Eucharistia*, I, 309.

[350] Cappello, *Tractatus Canonico-Moralis de Sacramentis*, I, 482; Noldin, *Theologia Moralis*, III, 173; Prümmer, *Theologia Moralis*, III, 152; Many, *Praelectiones de Missa cum Appendice de Sanctissimo Sacramento Eucharistiae*, p. 344; Vermeersch, *Theologia Moralis*, III, 316; Genicot, *Casus Conscientiae*, I, 225.

people as to why the priest was not able to celebrate the Holy Sacrifice, unless the priest is so very well known to his people, that he enjoys a reputation among them, that is beyond all danger of reproach and suspicion. If the priest were not to say Mass it can be easily understood how his parishioners might take this as an occasion to be less careful about the fulfillment of their Sunday obligation in the future. This is especially true in those regions where the faith at its best is not strong, and where the faithful have to come a long way for Mass.[351]

Furthermore, Vermeersch,[352] and Genicot[353] say, the word "scandal" in the response of the Holy Office is to be understood, not in its strict theological sense as an occasion of sin, but rather in the popular sense of astonishment or admiration. For, if there is present a real danger of scandal, then the natural law which forbids the giving of scandal takes precedence over the ecclesiastical law of the Eucharistic fast.

No hard and fast rule can be laid down to cover every case. The only principles which can be formulated are the following: 1) The mere admiration or wonderment on the part of the people is not a sufficient cause for the priest to feel excused from the law of fasting; 2) A priest may not say Mass after having broken his fast for the sole purpose that the faithful may fulfill their Sunday obligation; 3) The danger of scandal or the probable loss of reputation is a valid cause to justify the priest to say Mass after having broken his fast, provided of course that the celebration of the Mass would not of itself be a cause for scandal, as it would be if the faithful were aware of the fact that the priest had broken his fast. These principles would apply

[351] Nevin, "Duplicating after Fast Is Broken," *Australasian Catholic Record,* I, n. 3 (1924), 35-36; Tachy, "Etude Canonique et Liturgie sur le Binage," *Revue de Sciences Ecclésiastiques,* XLVII (1883), 510-514.

[352] *Theologia Moralis,* III, 256.

[353] *Casus Conscientiae,* II, 226.

not only on Sundays but even on week days if the required conditions of circumstances were verified.[354] However, since the same inconvenience or danger of scandal would not arise by the omission of Mass on a week-day, a priest should not be too hasty to believe that it does in a particular case. In practice it pertains to the individual priest to judge according to the accepted principles whether or not he would feel justified in saying a second Mass after having inadvertently broken his fast.

Danger of scandal or probable loss of reputation would excuse not only the priest but also a lay person, for instance, the communicant who was already at the altar rail when he recalled that he had broken his fast.

Akin to the danger of scandal or the probable loss of reputation is another cause, namely, very grave inconvenience. In general, most authors do not add this to the list of excusing causes, but treat it under the heading of scandal. In practice there are not many occasions when the inconvenience that would arise would be serious enough to warrant one either to say Mass or to receive Holy Communion after breaking one's fast. Some authors would allow a priest to celebrate Mass even though he were not fasting if he was threatened with the penalty of death if he did not celebrate, provided the celebration was not exacted in contempt of religion. The case is far fetched and it is difficult to conceive of it in the concrete, especially when some contempt of religion would not be involved.[355]

A more practical case is that of a newly ordained priest who inadvertently breaks his fast before his first public Mass. The inconvenience that might arise from the fact that the day and the hour of the Mass were announced and

[354] Cappello, *Tractatus Canonico-Moralis de Sacramentis*, I, 482.

[355] S. Alphonsus, *Theologia Moralis*, VI, n. 287; Tamburini, *Opera Omnia*, cap. II, ¶ 6, n. 45; La Croix, *Theologia Moralis*, II, lib. VI, dub. II, art. 2; Cappello, *Tractatus Canonico-Moralis de Sacramentis* I, 483.

all preparations were made for the occasion, in addition to the possible suspicion that might arise and the talk that would ensue seems to constitute a reasonable excuse for the young priest to assume that it would not be wrong for him to proceed with the Mass under such circumstances. He could not do so, however, if the fact that he had broken his fast had become known, since the celebration of the Holy Sacrifice of the Mass after people were aware that he had broken the Eucharistic fast, would prove a greater scandal.[356]

A somewhat similar case is that of a child on the day of its first solemn Communion or that of a betrothed couple on their wedding day. But the same inconvenience would not be present in these cases as in the instance of a newly ordained priest, and therefore one cannot argue the cases as being strictly *a pari*. The danger of scandal, or of inconvenience, would be extremely slight on the day of a child's first Communion day if for any reason he did not receive. For a newly married couple, especially in places where it is a very general custom for the bride and groom to receive Holy Communion at the nuptial Mass, there would be a greater danger of scandal and an occasion for malicious gossip, so that they might be allowed to receive Communion on that day even if they had accidentally broken the Eucharistic fast. However, since it would be so easy for abuses to arise on this score it is to be well borne in mind that the law of the Eucharistic fast is a very strict law subject to the strictest interpretation and that really serious reasons are required before one may rightly consider anyone exempt from it.

In all probability a priest would be allowed to say Mass to procure the Holy Viaticum for a dying person, if otherwise the person would be deprived of the consolation of the Blessed Sacrament at the hour of death. This ques-

[356] La Croix, *loc. cit.;* Noldin, *Theologia Moralis*, III, 153; Cappello, *Tractatus Canonico-Moralis de Sacramentis* I, 483.

tion is controverted among theologians. Saint Alphonsus calls the negative opinion the more common and also the more probable. The reason given by the defenders of this opinion are: 1) even though the precept of receiving Holy Viaticum is of divine origin and that of fasting is derived from a purely ecclesiastical law, nevertheless in substance the law of the Eucharistic fast also is divine because of the reverence due to the Blessed Sacrament, which reverence is not to be foregone for the sake of the sick since this sacrament is not of such great necessity; 2) the sick in such circumstances are not obliged to receive the Viaticum since it is not possible for them to do so except at the expense of a strict ecclesiastical law.[357]

The affirmative opinion has, however, become the more common one among modern authors. The defendants of this argue that the divine precept of receiving the Viaticum takes precedence over the ecclesiastical one of the Eucharistic fast. The added reason that if ecclesiastical law, precisely for the sake of providing Holy Communion to a dying person, allows him to receive Holy Viaticum without having observed the fast, then by the same token of a cogent solicitude for those who are about to die, the law of the Church can be interpreted as permitting a priest to celebrate Mass while not fasting, if such a celebration is the only means whereby this act of supreme charity can be realized for the dying person. St. Alphonsus acknowledged this affirmative opinion as being truly probable.[358] The more probable opinion today then is that a priest would be excused from the observance of the Eucharistic fast in order to say Mass, that he might procure the Holy Eucharist

[357] S. Alphonsus, *Theologia Moralis*, VI, 286; La Croix, *Theologia Moralis*, II, lib. VI, dub. II, art. 2; De Lugo *De Sacramento Eucharistiae*, disp. XV, sect. 2, n. 68; Many, *Praelectiones de Missa cum Appendice de Sanctissmo Sacramento Eucharistiae*, p. 342 Gasparri, *De Eucharistia*, I, 309.

[358] *Theologia Moralis*, VI, 286; *Cf.* also Suarez, *De Sacramento Eucharistiae*, disp. LXVIII, sect. 5, n. 5; Noldin, *Theologia Moralis*, III, 174; Cappello, *Tractatus Canonico-Moralis de Sacramentis*, I, 484.

to administer Viaticum. The reasons advanced by those who upheld the negative opinion and who insisted on the irreverence attached to celebration by a priest who had broken his fast do not carry much weight in the face of the actual fact that the Church nowadays so readily dispenses in the matter of the Eucharistic fast, when there is sufficient cause for this dispensation. Furthermore, the argument of the defenders of the negative opinion, that the sick are not obliged to receive Viaticum when it is not possible for them to do so except at the expense of a strict ecclesiastical law, practically amounts to an assertion that the fulfillment of a divine law may be conditioned by the Church upon the prior observance of an ecclesiastical law, over the fulfillment of which or concerning the violation of which, the dying persons themselves have no control. Moreover, the fact that there is no obligation for the dying to receive Holy Viaticum, when in order to procure the Blessed Sacment a nonfasting priest would have to celebrate Mass, should not be too strongly urged. Rather some thought should be given to the consideration that the dying should not be deprived of the great consolation which the Holy Eucharist affords them in the all-important and solemn moment of death.

Before the Decree *Post editum* of 1906,[359] which permitted the sick to receive Holy Communion under certain conditions even though they were not fasting, the question whether one who was not able to keep the Eucharistic fast could make use of epikeia in order to fulfill the Paschal precept was widely discussed. Subsequent to this decree, and due to the provision made in canon 858, ¶2, for those who have been confined to bed by illness for a month, the question is now of small practical import. However, in an unusual case wherein a person finds it impossible to fast, and at the same time does not fall under the category of the sick mentioned in canon 858, ¶2, he would probably be permitted to receive

[359] S. C. C., decr., 7 dec. 1906—*Fontes*, n. 4331.

Holy Communion at the time of Easter to fulfill the Pascal precept, since the obligation to receive Holy Communion during the Paschal season is of Divine ecclesiastical origin, and is therefore to be more strongly urged than the ecclesiastical law of fasting. Care, however, must be taken lest this benign interpretation of the mind of the law giver become the occasion of any irreverence, abuse or scandal.[360]

A few words can be added here in the manner of a corollary concerning the law of the Eucharistic fast and children, who though not seven years of age, have come to the use of reason and have been admitted to first Holy Communion. Are they obliged to observe the ecclesiastical law of the Eucharistic fast?

The question can be considered under a twofold aspect, namely, as a juridical problem, or as a moral issue. From a moral point of view, which demands more than what is required by the strict letter of the law, children under seven should observe the law of the Eucharistic fast, since they should be accustomed from a tender age to obey the laws of the Church, when this is reasonably possible. Moreover, if children are allowed to receive Holy Communion while not fasting before the age of seven, they might be led to believe that the precept of the Eucharistic fast is an arbitrary obligation, and be inclined to be careless in the observance of the Eucharistic fast after they have reached the age of seven years. There might also be present a danger of scandal for other children, who seeing children under seven years of age allowed to receive Holy Communion while not fasting, might not understand why this exception should be made.

Considering the question in its juridical aspects it is certain that children under seven years of age are not bound to the observance of the Eucharistic fast. Canon 12 states that children under seven years of age are not bound to

[360] Cappello, *Tractatus Canonico-Moralis de Sacramentis*, I, 485; Gasparri, *De Eucharistia*, II, 361.

observe ecclesiastical laws, though they actually have the use of reason, unless the Code explicitly subjects them to some particular law. Canon 858, ¶1, prescribes that those who have not kept the natural fast from midnight may not be admitted to the reception of the Holy Eucharist. This latter canon does not explicitly mention children under seven years of age as subjects of the law of the Eucharistic fast. Hence, the whole matter may be reduced to this: Is the law of the Eucharistic fast a purely ecclesiastical law? Historically it has been proven that it is purely an ecclesiastical precept, which was unknown in the very early ages of the Church. It is likewise the unanimous opinion of theologians and canonists that the obligation of the natural fast arises from a mere ecclesiastical regulation. Therefore, according to the principles of the Code, and in the strict letter of the law, children under seven years of age, who have been admitted to their first Holy Communion, are not obliged to the observance of the natural fast, which is prescribed in canon 858, ¶1.[361]

361 ". . .infans. . .in rigore iuris non tenetur servare ieiunii eucharisticum praeceptum, quippe quod sit mere ecclesiasticum."—Prümmer, *Theologia Moralis*, I, 127; 'Questions des Sciences Ecclesiastiques," *L'Ami du Clerge*, XLVI (1929), 88-89.

CHAPTER IV

THE COMMUNION OF THE SICK

On December 20, 1905, His Holiness, Pope Pius X, issued through the Sacred Congregation of the Council the solemn Decree *Sacred Tridentina Synodus,* in which he reasserted the right of all the faithful respecting the frequent reception of Holy Communion. Thus an end was put to the arduous question which had been so long disputed among theologians on the necessary dispositions for frequent or daily Communion. The Decree, addressed to all the bishops of the Church awakened the interest of the entire Catholic world in regard to the necessity of a more frequent reception of Our Lord in the Blessed Sacrament.[362]

Some time after this decree a Belgian priest raised the question of a modification of the general law of fasting before Communion in favor of the sick so that they might be permitted to receive Holy Communion without the obligation of observing the Eucharistic fast. Up until this time the law had been that only those who were in danger of death were allowed to receive Communion while not fasting. The matter was brought to Rome and discussed in the Sacred Congregation of the Council. Arguments *pro* and *con* were brought forth. The reasons which were alleged against the proposed change of discipline were: 1) that the words of the ritual were opposed to it; 2) that it would increase parochial duties to too great an extent, and tend to diminish the reverence shown to the Blessed Sacrament when it was carried to the sick; 3) that individual dispensations were sufficient to meet the exigencies of the case.

[362] *Sacra Tridentina Synodus,* 20 dec. 1905—*AAS,* II (1910), 894.

In favor of a modification it was urged: 1) that in the case of the sick there was no danger of the abuses which the general law was intended to repress; 2) it was rather anomalous that the very class which needed the consolation of the Blessed Eucharist most, should in many cases be all but deprived of it; 3) that the law was merely an ecclesiastical one and should yield to the spiritual needs of the faithful and to the right to receive the Eucharist as warranted for them by the recent decree.[363]

After mature consideration, Pope Pius X who has rightly been called the "Pope of the Eucharist" issued through the Sacred Congregation of the Council the decree *"Post editum"* of December 7, 1906, making it possible for the sick to receive Holy Communion with relative frequency. The concession granted by the decree was to the effect that the sick who had been confined to bed for a month and who furnished no hope of a speedy recovery and moreover, were not able to keep the natural fast but found it necessary to take some liquid food before Communion, were nevertheless allowed to receive Holy Communion. The decree provided that they might receive once or twice a month if they were living in their own homes, once or twice a week if they lived in a religious house, hospital or place in which the Blessed Sacrament was habitually reserved, or if they enjoyed the privilege of having Mass in a domestic Oratory.[364]

As soon as this decree was issued, commentators immediately questioned the literal sense of the word *decumbentes*. Was it to be referred to only those who were actually bed-ridden, or was it to be accepted in a wider sense, so that those who were sick, though not actually confined to

363 "De SS. Communione puerorum nuper ad S. Synaxim admissorum, necnon infirmorum morbo chronico laborantium et naturale ieiunium servare non valentium," *ASS*, XXXIX (1906), 499-510; "Causes Jugées dans la Séance du Sept. 1906," *Le Canoniste Contemporain*, XXX (1907), 34-40; Kinane, "The Eucharistic Fast—The Decree of 1906; What Class of Persons Are Affected?" *IER*, 5 series, III, (1914), 416-420.

364 S. C. C., decr. 7 dec. 1906—*Fontes*, n. 4331.

bed, might also be made the beneficiaries of this concession. The doubt was proposed in Rome and a response of the Sacred Congregation of the Council declared that the term *decumbentes* included not only those who were habitually confined to their beds but also embraced those who, on account of the nature of their sickness could not remain in bed, and those who were able to be up for a few hours each day, provided the physician judged that they could not keep the natural fast.[365] This response was confirmed by His Holiness, Pope Pius X.

The concession granted to the sick in 1906 is now contained in the Code. "The sick who have been confined to bed for a month without certain hope of a speedy recovery may, with the prudent advice of the confessor, receive Holy Communion once or twice a week though they have taken medicine, or some liquid food beforehand."[366]

The difference between the privilege granted in the original Decree and that stated in the Code may be noted. According to the Code no distinction is made between the sick who are living at home and those who are in a religious house, hospital, or place in which the Blessed Sacrament is reserved, or those who enjoy the privilege of having Mass in a domestic oratory. Likewise, the privilege as it was originally granted allowed that only some liquid food might be taken before Communion. The Code has further granted that medicine may also be taken, whether it is liquid or solid, since the term *medicine* in the canon is not in any manner limited.

From the wording of the canon it is evident that not all sick persons may enjoy this privilege, but only those who are in the circumstances described in the canon, namely, the sick who have been confined to bed for a month or more. Hence, those who are not sick, even though they may

365 S. C. C., 6 mart. 1907—*AAS*, XL (1907), 344.
366 Canon 858, ¶ 2.

not be able to go to Church, or may not be able to observe the natural fast, cannot avail themselves of this favor. The question is whether the words of the canon *infirmi qui iam a mense decumbunt* are to be taken in a strict literal sense so that they include only those who are habitually obliged to remain in bed, or whether they may be taken in a wider sense to embrace those who are described in the extensive Declaration of the Decree of 1906, namely those who because of the peculiar nature of their sickness cannot remain in bed or who are able to be up for only a few hours each day? The answer will depend on the relation which the Declaration defining the term *decumbentes* had to the original Decree of 1906.

Woywod considers this Declaration as an extension of the original Decree. He says that this is indicated by the fact that the phrase "*Facto verbo cum sanctissimo ad cautelam*" was employed. Hence, he concludes that the extension of the term "*decumbunt*" cannot be applied to the Code. His opinion is that the Decree of December 7, 1906, and its Declaration are not law any longer, since the Code does not repeat the former decree in its entirety, but makes several important changes. He concludes that if a dispensation from the Eucharistic fast is necessary for persons who are sick and not confined to bed, and their sickness is according to the judgment of the physician such that they cannot without danger keep the fast, application for a dispensation may be made to the Apostolic Delegate.[367]

It is true that for some unknown reason the Declaration of 1907 is not given as a reference in the Code among the sources of canon 858, ¶2. However, since it was an authentic interpretation of the Decree of 1906, it seems with good reason that the scope of this Declaration is not foreign to the Code. Even though this Declaration were an extension of the former Decree, it might still be considered as leaving its imprint on canon 858, ¶2. The canon repeats the iden-

[367] *A Practical Commentary on the Code of Canon Law,* I, 411.

tical words of the Decree, *"infirmi qui decumbunt"*. Hence, if these words were given a more extensive meaning than the force of the words themselves implied in order to define more specificly those whom the Church wished to make the beneficiaries of this privilege, and if this same privilege is indeed granted in the Code, then there is a strong presumption that the Church still intends to extend the meaning of the words *"infirmi qui decumbunt"* to the same category of the sick in whose favor this concession was granted in the Declaration. Practically all authors maintain that the scope of the Declaration can be appropriated in the interpretation of canon 858, ¶2.[368]

The question must be regulated according to the rules laid down in the first six canons of the Code which govern the change of discipline from the old law to the new law now embodied in the Code. With regard to the former law, canon 6 states in general that as a rule the old discipline is to be retained, though there are indeed some modifications of the old law. Number 3 of the same canon states that those canons which agree only in part with the former law must be interpreted according to the old law in the part in which they agree with the former law; in the parts which differ from the old law, the canons must be interpreted according to the meaning of the words employed. Number 4 of canon 6 ordains that in case of doubt whether some provision of the canon differs from the old law, one must adhere to the old law. The former law thus continues to be at least implicitly contained in the Code, and thus retains its force as law, in as much as canon 6, number 6, points to the repeal of only such disciplinary law which is neither *explicitly* nor *implicitly* reassumed in the Code.

Canon 858, ¶2, repeats at least in part the Decree of 1906. Hence, in that part in which it agrees with this former law

[368] Cappello, *Tractatus Canonico-Moralis de Sacramentis*, I, 474; Jorio, *La Comunione Agl' Infermi*, p. 42; Vermeersch-Creusen, *Epitome Iuris Canonici*, II, 86; Darmanin, "La Comunione Agli Infermi non Digiuni," *Monitore Ecclesiastico*, 5 series, IV (1932), 132.

it must be interpreted according to the old law, that is, it should be given the same sense and extension which the original Decree enjoyed. By reason of the authentic Declaration of 1907 the words of the Decree of 1906 had a much greater extension than they originally had. Hence, this Declaration is implicitly contained in the present law embodied in canon 858, ¶2. Thus it still has the force of law. Therefore, the tenor of canon 858, ¶2, is that the sick who have been confined to bed for a month and for whom there is no hope of a speedy recovery, or also those who because of the nature of their sickness cannot remain in bed or who are able to arise for only a few hours each day, but who find it impossible to observe the natural fast, may, with the prudent advice of the confessor, receive Holy Communion once or twice a week, even though they may have taken medicine or some liquid food beforehand.[369]

The canon does not require any specified illness nor does it mention any degree of the gravity of the sickness which would suffice in order that one would be privileged by this concession. Since the law does not demand a grave illness, even a slight sickness would excuse from the obligation of the fast, *servatis servandis,* provided that the sickness was of such a nature than it confined the person to bed or placed him in the circumstances described in the Declaration of 1907. As Cappello observes, generally when a person is confined to bed he is laboring under a grave illness. Nevertheless it sometimes happens that a person is only slightly ill and yet finds it necessary to remain in bed in order to secure the necessary rest and to allay any further aggravation of the illness. In these circumstances may one make use of the indult of canon 858, ¶2.[370] The wording of the canon offers no reason why they could not. Therefore, any one who is confined to bed by illness, whatever may

[369] Darmanin, "La Comunione Agli Infermi non Digiuni," *Monitore Ecclesiastico,* 5 series, IV (1932), 133; Kinane, "Some Queries in Regard to the Modification of the Eucharistic Fast for the Sick," IER, XXXV (1930), 519-521.

[370] Tractatus *Canonico-Moralis de Sacramentis,* I, 468.

be the origin or the nature of the illness or the degree of its gravity, may make use of the indult. However, since the canon demands an illness, it follows that one who is prevented from leaving the house by some accident or incapacity would not be considered by that very fact exempt from the law of fasting.

While a slight illness would suffice to excuse one from the general law, if this illness made it necessary for him to remain in bed, yet it seems that this would not be true if the sick person was able to be up and around all day. The doubt which was proposed to the Sacred Congregation of the Council, and the response of the Congregation in answer to the doubt explicitly mentions those who are afflicted with a *grave* illness, but who because of the nature of their sickness cannot remain in bed. Wherefore, in order that the sick who are not confined to bed may be classed among those who are dispensed in virtue of canon 858, ¶2, not every sickness suffices, but it is necessary that it be a grave infirmity. The gravity of the illness may be determined according to the judgment of the physician, or according to the estimation in the light of which an illness is generally considered grave or slight by the common consent of men. Darmanin stresses the distinction between the sick who cannot remain in bed and the sick who are able not to remain in bed. It is the difference between *decumbere non possunt* and *non decumbere possunt*. Hence, even in giving the words "*non decumbentes*" a wide interpretation, this distinction must be taken into consideration.[371]

The same may also be said of those who, though they be sick, are able to rise for a few hours each day. In their case likewise a grave illness is required. Nor can the words of the declaration, "*Aut ex eo* (*lecto*) *aliquibus horis diei surgere queunt,*" be interpreted in such a wide sense that they would include those who are ailing but nevertheless are not

[371] "La Comunione Agli' Infermi non Digiuni," *Monitore Ecclesiastico,* 5 series, IV (1932), 178-179.

confined to bed and are able to be up throughout the whole day. Even in a wide interpretation the proper and real meaning of the words of the law must be maintained. Hence, those persons who are suffering from minor stomach ailments or who are in the first stages of tuberculosis, of cancer, and of other malignant diseases, which may prevent them from attending to their daily occupations, but which are not sufficiently serious to make it necessary for them habitually to take to their bed, cannot be classed as sick (*infirmi*) in the sense in which this term is used in canon 858, ¶2. Anyone who finds himself in this situation and for whom there is a particular difficulty in observing the Eucharistic fast can apply for a dispensation which will be readily granted. This conclusion is entirely in agreement with a response given by the Sacred Congregation of the Sacraments on November 22, 1909, in answer to a doubt which was proposed, namely, whether the sick who are constantly ill, but who are not sick in bed, were comprehended in the Decree of 1906. The answer was given in the negative. The Sacred Congregation ruled that recourse must be had for a dispensation in the individual case.[372]

Cappello says that the circumstance that the sick person is actually confined to bed is merely accidental, since the sickness is to be considered primarily and as a *conditio sine qua non,* for he says one may be afflicted with a serious illness, such as cancer, and not be able to lie still in bed, while another who is afflicted with a less serious disease may be forced to remain in bed. Why should this favor be granted to the latter and denied to the former? For where there is the same reason there should be the same disposition of law.[373]

The privilege granted in canon 858, ¶2, is given relative

[372] Jorio, *La Comunione Agl' Infermi,* p. 43. This response does not appear in the *Acta* or the *Fontes.* It must have been a private answer. Jorio cites it but does not give any source for it.
[373] *Tractatus Canonico-Moralis de Sacramentis,* I, 474.

to the reception of Holy Communion, and not for the celebration of Mass. Formerly, it was practically accepted as a principle among theologians that it was lawful for a priest to say Mass without fasting whenever he found the circumstances to be such as permitted a lay person to receive Holy Communion without observing the fast.[374] This principle, however, cannot be applied in the present case. In the first place, since the celebration of the Holy Sacrifice of the Mass is the greatest act of Christian worship, there is a greater bond between the celebrant and the act of celebrating Mass than there is between the communicant and the act of receiving Holy Communion. For this reason it cannot be argued that by the very fact that a dispensation is given to receive Communion non-fasting, it can be extended to allow the celebration of Mass while one is not fasting. Moreover, the privilege granted by the Decree *Post editum*, and reaffirmed in the Code was given in order that those who by reason of their sickness could not keep the natural fast might not be entirely deprived of the great benefits of the Blessed Sacrament. To be sure a priest who is ill may enjoy this privilege by receiving Holy Communion after the manner of the laity, but he may not make use of it to say Mass after having broken his fast.[375] While the term *infirmi* (sick) seems to presuppose that the persons in question are confined to bed, or are at least compelled to remain always in their room or in the house, yet in a particular case it may happen that persons who are ill in the sense of the word in which *infirmi* is used in the Code, will be able to go to the parish Church, *v.g.*, a person with a grave heart ailment who because of his illness cannot remain in bed, and who is able to be driven in a machine each morn-

[374] S. Alphonsus, *Theologia Moralis*, VI, 286: "Non plus est celebrare, quam communicare sumpto cibo."; De Lugo, *De Sacramento Eucharistiae*, dist. XV, sect. 4.

[375] Cappello, *Tractatus Canonico-Moralis de Sacramentis*, I, 477; Tummolo-Jorio, *Compendium Theologiae Moralis* (5 ed., 2 vols., Neapoli: 1935), II, 220; Kinane, "Celebration of Mass by a Priest Excused from Fasting," *IER*, 5 series, IX (1917), 225; Mahoney, "The Eucharistic Fast," *The Clergy Review*, IV (1932) 70.

ing to the parish Church. Could they in this case receive Holy Communion while not fasting, by making use of the privilege of canon 858, ¶2? In all probability they could. This is especially true if there be question of persons who are living in a religious house, hospital, or institution, where there is a chapel or oratory. Since they are allowed to make use of the indult even though they are able to be up out of bed for a few hours during the day, this privilege should not be denied to them because of the fact that they are able to go to a church or chapel.[376]

The whole question in regard to those who may be called *infirmi* in the sense in which it is used in canon 858, ¶2, may be summed up in a few lines. The following may make use of the privilege 1) Those who are habitually confined to bed by their illness, whether or not their illness is grave, and independently of the nature or origin of their sickness. 2) Those who because of the peculiar nature of their sickness cannot remain in bed, provided that in the judgment of their physician their illness is grave. 3) Those who are seriously ill, but who are able to be up for a few hours each day.

Canon 858, ¶2, further requires that one must have been sick *for a month* in order to make use of this privilege. According to the general norms laid down in the first book of the Code for the reckoning of time, a month is understood to designate a period of thirty days, unless the law states that the month is to be computed as a calendar month.[377] Canon 34 determines when the one or the other of the two computations is to be used. A month is to be computed according to the calendar or if it is designated by its own proper name, or in equivalent words; if the period of time comprises a continuous or uninterrupted duration; and if

[376] Cappello, *Tractatus Canonico-Moralis de Sacramentis*, I, 475; Jorio, *La Comunione Agl' Infermi*, p. 43; *Ferreres, Razon y Fe*, XVII (1907), 240; "The Eucharistic Fast," *The Clergy Review*, III (1932), 145-146.

[377] Canon 32, ¶ 2.

the time or period consists of one or more months, and the starting point is explicitly or implicitly determined. In these hypotheses the duration of the time would differ according to the various months and would range anywhere from twenty-eight to thirty-one days.[378]

The *terminus a quo* is the initial moment from which the computation in question is to be reckoned. This *terminus a quo* is determined if the beginning of the period of time allotted for anything is specified or indicated by designating the moment from which the said period of time has its starting point. This determination of the time can be specified in the law itself or by the lawgiver. This designation may be either explicit or implicit. It is explicit when it is expressly indicated, *e.g.*, two months vacation from the fifteenth of June. The determination is implicit when although it is not expressly stated in law, it may nevertheless be implied from the wording of the law together with the circumstances of the case, or from the nature of the matter under consideration. For example, if a clause in the law, indicating the time set for a certain action, presupposes from the very nature of the matter, the day on which the act is to have its beginning, v.g., ten days to appeal, or within eight days from the notice of the vacancy of the episcopal see.

The starting point is neither implicitly nor explicity determined if the *terminus a quo* depends solely on the will of the person to whom the period of time in question is allotted, v.g., two months vacation during the year.

The Code states in a more detailed manner that if the *terminus a quo* is explicitly or implicitly determined, and in reality coincides with the beginning of the day, the first day in its entirety is counted in reckoning the time, and the final moment of the allotted period of a month will be reached with the beginning of that day which in the fol-

[378] Canon 34, ¶ 1, 2, 3.

lowing calendar month bears an identical date with that of the initial day. If in a similar determination of the starting point the latter is not coincident with the beginning of the day, then no part of the first day is included in the reckoning, and the month will expire with the end of that day which in the following calendar month is of the same date as that of the initial day. If the following month lacks an identical date, as in the case when the month begins to elapse from January thirtieth, then the calendar month will be completed either with the beginning or with the end of the last day of the following month, in accordance respectively with the inclusion or exclusion of the day which marked the starting point for the month's duration.[379]

For determining the duration of a month's illness which computation is to be used? Many authors do not explain the term "month" as it is used in canon 858, ¶2. Woywod, Augustine, Noldin, and Ferreres do no treat the question. Those who do enter into an explanation of it widely disagree in their opinion. Prümmer says, "*A triginta diebus.*"[380] Darmanin contends that the month here should be taken according to the calendar, because according to canon 34, ¶3, n. 1, a month is to be computed as a calendar month when the *terminus a quo* is explicitly or implicity assigned. Furthermore, he adds that even in the supposition that the starting point is not implicitly or explicitly determined by law, the month's illness should be reckoned as a calendar month, because according to canon 34, ¶2, if the lapse of time is continuous the month and year are to be taken as they are in the calendar. Hence, he says, a month's illness includes all and only those days which elapse from that day on which the illness had its beginning and ends on the same date in the month immediately following, so that it is not necessary to count the

379 Canon 34, ¶2, ¶3, nn. 2, 3, 4.
380 *Theologia Moralis*, III, 153.

number of days in the interim. For instance, if one were taken ill on the thirtieth or the thirty-first of January the month would be completed on the last day of February.[381]

Jorio formerly was of the same opinion as Darmanin, namely, that the month should be taken according to the calendar. He also maintained that the rules governing the reckoning of time in regard to cases in which the *terminus a quo* coincides or does not coincide with the beginning of the day, should be applied in determining the duration of a month's illness. He observed that the sick person is not obliged to make this calculation, but that it is left to the judgment of the confessor.[382] However, in a more recent work he says that while the month of which there is question in canon 858, ¶2, *per se* should be computed as a calendar month in accordance with the prescript of canon 34, ¶2, nevertheless for a just and reasonable cause, it may be reckoned morally, i.e., a period of twenty-six or twenty-seven days. The reason he gives for this is that many authors interpreted the month in a moral sense, when the concession of non-fasting Communion was first granted to the sick by the decree *"Post editum"* in 1906.[383]

Cappello considers that the month in this case need not be taken with canonical and mathematical precision. According to him the month in this instance may be taken in a moral sense, so that a defect of a few days could be neglected. He cites a response of the Pontifical Commission for the Interpretation of the Code to this effect. The Code Commission was asked: "Whether the month's illness mentioned in canon 858, ¶2, is to be computed mathematically, or rather morally." The reply was given: "In the negative."

[381] "La Comunione Agli Infermi non Digiuni," *Monitore Ecclesiastico*, 5 series, V (1933), 170-174; 242-246.
[382] *La Comunione Agl' Infermi*, pp. 38-40.
[383] Tummulo-Jorio, *Compendium Theologiae Moralis*, II.

to the first part; in the affirmative to the second part."[384]

[384] (Private) PCI, 24 nov. 1927—*Periodica*, XXIII, (1934), 234; Bouscaren, *Canon Law Digest*, II, 88.

To this he adds a further argument gathered from the purpose of the law, the spirit and mind of the Church, and a consideration of the interpretation which was given to the term "month" in the old law.[385]

Vermeersch in his Moral Theology and in his Epitome of Canon Law understood the month as a period of thirty days. However, in an article which appeared in the *Periodica* he renounced his previous opinion and held that it sufficed that the sick person be confined to bed for thirty days morally speaking, *i.e.*, for a period of twenty-six or twenty-seven days.[386]

In such a divergency of opinions which one is to be followed? In the attempt to reach a solution of the problem, it must be borne in mind that it is not here a question of a strict juridical issue, but rather of a moral matter. Hence, in the place of a juridical reckoning of the term "month" in accordance with the prescripts of canon 34, we feel that one would be justified in making use of a less strict interpretation of canon 858, ¶2, and adopting a moral computation of the term "*a mense*" as it is used in this same canon.

If the word "month" is taken as its stands in canon 858, ¶2, in connection with canon 34, with canonical precision, and independently of any other consideration, we have to agree with Darmanin that a month's illness must be reckoned according to the calendar since the starting point or *terminus a quo* is implicitly determined through the circumstances which marks the beginning of the month's illness. Not only would this general rule apply, but so also would the norms which are enacted to determine the exact time when a month would be completed in accordance with whether or not the *terminus a quo* coincided with the begin-

385 *Tractatus Canonico-Moralis de Sacramentis*, I, 464-468.

386 "Recta Computatio Mensis, Quo Elapso, Licet Semel vel Bis in Hebedomada, Decumbenti Infirmo Permittere ut S. Dape Reficiatur Postquam Aliquid per Modum Potus vel Medicinae Sumpserit," *Periodica*, XXIII (1934), 61*-63*.

ning of the day. In this supposition a month would be any number of days from the twenty-eight to thirty-one.

It may be objected that if the starting point for the lapse of a given period of time is connected with a contingent event, such as sickness, over which neither man nor the law has any control, that the *terminus a quo* of such a period of time cannot be either explicitly or implicitly assigned in law. We answer that even in this case the law can designate the *terminus a quo*—to be sure, not in the sense that it predetermines the initial moment of a month's illness, but it stipulates that after a person has been sick for a month, the sick person may make use of the privilege of canon 858, ¶2. The fact that in canon 858, ¶2, it is question of a period of time which has already transpired, shows clearly how the legislator could designate the *terminus a quo* of such a period of time, even though this *terminus a quo* is connected with a contingent event. It is precisely because it is a contingent event over which the sick person in question has no control, that it cannot be said that it is left to himself to designate the starting point of the requisite given period of time, which is necessary in accordance with the ruling of canon 858, ¶2, before one may make use of the privilege which is granted to the sick to receive Holy Communion while not fasting. Independent of the will of the sick person the month's illness has its starting point on the first day that he is taken ill. Hence, when the Code says, "*one who has been confined to bed for a month by illness,*" it at least implicitly, if not explicitly, specifies that the period of a month's illness has its starting point from the day or moment on which a person is compelled to take to his bed because of illness.

This conclusion, however, that a month's illness must be computed as a calendar month, is a solution which is given in all canonical rigor, and presupposes that there is no doubt whatsoever in what sense, moral or juridical, the month mentioned in canon 858, ¶2, is to be taken. Evidently there is some doubt, as the difference of opinion among authors indicates. According to canon 18, ecclesiastical laws are to be understood according to the proper meaning of the words considered in their text and context; if there are still doubts, recourse is to be had to parallel passages of the Code, if there are any, and to the purposes of the law and the mind of the legislator. Canon 6, n. 2, also states that the canons which repeat the old law in its entirety are to be interpreted according to the old law and the interpretation of approved authors. Number 4 in the same canon rules that in doubt whether or not the prescripts of the Code differ from the old law, the old law is to be maintained.

Now, the interpretation of the words "*a mense*" in canon 858 in a mathematical sense would practically render the law very difficult, if not altogether impossible. According to such an interpretation it would be necessary to enter into numerous computations regarding the exact time of day when a person was taken ill. In the common ordinary cases which the priest encounters in his ministry this would be next to impossible. It would expose the priest and the faithful to numerous doubts and anxieties. Surely, the Legislator, who understands that things are done in a human manner, could not have intended this. It is not a question here of reckoning time relative to juridical issues such as is the case in the inflicting of penalties, in the exercise of one's rights or in the placing of juridical acts, but it is only a question of a moral matter, namely, of the use of a general privilege granted by law.

Before the Code there were not the same definite norms for the reckoning of time, as there are now given in the Code. Pre-Code authors, interpreting the term "*a mense*" as it was used in the Decree *Post editum* of 1906, held that the month's duration could be computed according to a month's moral reckoning.[387] Canon 858, ¶2, repeats the

[387] Van Hove, *De Consuetudine, de Temporis Supputatione*, n. 273, 275; D'Annibale, *Summula Theologiae Moralis* (5 ed.; 3 vols., Romae:

words "*a mense*" of the Decree of 1906 verbatim. Canon 6 rules that those canons which restate the old law without change, must be explained according to the old law, and according to the interpretation given by approved authors, that is, according to the former teaching and jurisprudence. If we interpret the term "*a mense*" according to the old law and the accepted interpretation of approved authors, as is prescribed by canon 6, it can be cancluded that the month mentioned in canon 858, ¶2, may be understood in a moral sense. Moreover, the purpose of the law and the mind of the Church was evidently to give those who were sick an opportunity of receiving Holy Communion even though they were not able to keep the fast. A month was considered a relatively long time for them to be deprived of the benefit of the Holy Eucharist. To preclude any longer deprival the privilege of receiving Holy Communion while not fasting was granted to them. In view of this purpose it would seem an undue solicitude for the letter of the law to deprive sick persons of this privilege for the sole reason that they have been ill for only twenty-seven or twenty-eight days instead of twenty-nine or thirty, which would be required to complete the month if it was reckoned according to the calendar. It may be objected that this attitude implies an utter disregard of the sacred canons and of canonical interpretation. This objection is without foundation. The interpretation of the words "*a mense*" in canon 858, ¶2, in their text and context, are not altogether clear. The general norms for the interpretation of the canons prescribe that in doubt recourse is to be had to the old law and to the interpretation of pre-Code

1908), I, 31, footnote 9; Vermeersch, "Recta Computatio Mensis, Quo Elapso, Licet Semel vel Bis in Hebdomada, Decumbenti Infermo Permittere ut S. Dape Reficiatur Postquam Aliquid per Modum Potus vel Medicinae Sumpserit,"—*Periodica*, XXIII (1934), 61*-63*; De Smet, *Collationes Brugenses*, XII (1907) 136; Bastien, cited in *Periodica*, III (1907), 179; Cappello, "Num Mensis, de Quo in Canone 858, ¶2, Sit Moraliter Sumendus, an Potius Mathematice," *Periodica*, XXIII (1934), 61*, 234* sq.; Tummulo-Jorio, *Compendium Theologiae Moralis*, II, 219.

authors. Finally an unofficial decision of the Code Commission throws some weight in favor of reckoning the month's illness in a moral sense. Since this reply of the Commission was private, and did not appear in the Acta Apostolicae Sedis, it has not the force of law. However, it is an indication of the mind of the Commission on the question, and shows that they were aware of the obvious difficulty in reckoning the month mathematically.[388] A consideration of these arguments, along with the fact that some eminent canonists are of the opinion that the month in question should be computed morally, leads to the conclusion that it is sufficient if a person has been sick for twenty-six or twenty-seven days in order to make use of the privilege granted in canon 658, ¶2.

In all probability one who has been sick in a morally continuous way for the duration of a month could be allowed to make use of the indult of canon 858, ¶2. For instance, one who has been confined to bed by sickness for many days of the month, but has during that period of time enjoyed a few days of better health, could in all probability avail himself of the privilege. These few days would not have to be deducted in reckoning the number of days required for a month's illness, nor would the month's duration have to be considered broken by the fact that a few days intervened on which the person enjoyed good health. Since the faculty granted in canon 858, ¶2, is a privilege, it receives a wide interpretation. Moreover, the canon does not say *qui a mense continuo decumbunt,* but merely "*qui a mense decumbunt*".[389]

However, the fact that it is forseen that a person will be confined to bed for a month would not warrant the use of

[388] Cappello, *Tractatus Canonico-Moralis de Sacramentis,* I, 464-468; Bouscaren, *Canon Law Digest,* II, 88; Vermeersch, *op. cit.,* 61*; Cappello, "De Facultate Concessa Infirmis ex Canone 858, ¶ 2," *Periodica,* XXIV (1935), 18*; "The Eucharistic Fast," *The Clergy Review,* XVI (1938), 253; Tummulo-Jorio, *loc. cit.*

[389] Vermeersch, *op. cit.,* 63*.

this privilege before a month had actually transpired. The Code says "*Qui iam a mense,*" which denotes that a month has already elapsed. Furthermore, the faculty is given to Nuncios and Internuncios for the place of their mission, and to Apostolic Delegates for their jurisdictions, of granting the privilege of receiving Holy Communion once a week to the sick who are confined to bed and for whom there is no certain hope of a speedy convalescence, even before the end of the month's illness. Likewise, Ordinaries in mission countries have the faculty of granting the privilege in virtue of which the sick may receive Holy Communion while not fasting two or three times a week even before the end of the month's illness. If it is question of priests or religious, they may grant them this privilege to receive Holy Communion daily while not fasting.[390] These faculties would be superfluous, if it were true that the sick could enjoy this privilege because it was foreseen that they would be confined to bed for a month.

The sick of whom there is question in canon 858, ¶2, may not receive every day without fasting, but only *once or twice* a week. The words "once or twice" are to be interpreted strictly to mean once or at most twice in the same week. No priest would be justified in allowing sick persons to receive Holy Communion more often than this if they were not fasting.

If however, a sick person could fast for receiving on other days during the week, he or she would still be able to make use of the privilege of receiving once or twice a week without observing the fast. As Augustine says, paragraph two of canon 858, is a positive grant or permission which the law giver undoubtedly wishes to see made use of in order

[390] Index Facultatum Quas, pro Locis Missionis suae, Nuntiis, Internuntiis et Delegatis Apostolicis Penes Civitates seu Nationes, Post Codicis Iuris Canonici Publicationem Tribuere SSus Dominus Noster Decrevit, Ceteris Abrogatis, cap. IV, n. 42—Vermeersch-Creusen, *Epitome Iuris Canonici,* I, 634; Formulae Facultatum Quas S. C. de Prop. Fide Ordinariis in Terris Missionum Procurat, n. 17—Vermeersch-Creusen, *Epitome Iuris Canonici,* I, 642.

to foster the frequency of Holy Communion. However, there would be no grant or favor conveyed by canon 858 if the persons in this case would not be permitted to receive once or twice a week, supposing they had already received in compliance with paragraph one of the same canon.[391]

The Code requires that in order to make use of the permission the sick should seek the prudent advice of the confessor. It does not demand the advice of the pastor or a chaplain or of the sick person's regular confessor. This is in keeping with the general principle that the confessor is the one who is qualified to judge of the presence of the disposition required for the reception of Holy Communion. It is the duty of the priest whose advice is sought to judge of the dispositions of the person, to inquire if the requisite conditions are verified in the case, to instruct the communicant as to the number of times he is permitted to receive Communion while not fasting, and to tell him that he is allowed to take only some medicine or something in liquid form before he is to receive Holy Communion. Since the Code demands that consultation with the confessor be undertaken before the grant of canon 858, ¶2, is called into use, this advice should be sought. While the Code demands only the advice of the confessor, and not his consent yet it would be very imprudent, to say the least, for a lay person not to ask the advice of the confessor in this matter. With far greater reason it appears that a lay person would not be free of all moral blame if he were to override the judgment of the confessor, and contrary to his counsel receive Holy Communion without observing the fast.

The words *with the prudent advice of the confessor* do not signify that the confessor himself grants any dispensation to the sick. He merely declares that in the circumstances it would be permissible according to law for the sick person to make use of the grant. Wherefore, a priest or re-

391 Augustine, *A Commentary on Canon Law*, IV, 236; Vermeersch-Creusen, *Epitome Iuris Canonici*, II, 87; Cappello, *op. cit.*, 30*.

ligious who is conscious of having the necessary dispositions and who can rightly judge of the conditions demanded in canon 858, ¶2, may even without the advice of the confessor, make use of the privilege.[392] Likewise if a patient, *e.g.*, a priest, would know that the confessor is handling the case without prudent counsel, *v.g.*, by allowing the reception of Holy Communion to him while not fasting more often than twice a week, the sick priest would be bound not to yield to the imprudent disposition which the confessor makes in the case, since it is not within the power of the confessor to extend the use of this privilege beyond the limits which are stated in law.

According to the conditions of the favor granted in canon 858, ¶2, only medicine or some liquid food may be taken by the sick before Holy Communion. Medicine, according to the common meaning of the word is that which directly tends to the healing of some illness. The medicine may be either liquid or solid. The Decree of 1906 did not contain the words *"aliquam medicinam"*. Their insertion in the Code is a further extension of the original grant, and there is no foundation for saying that this phrase in canon 858,¶2, is modified by the words *"per modum potus"*.[393]

This phrase *"aliquid per podum potus"* includes broth, coffee, and any other liquid food. It is permissible to mix solid substances with the liquid, provided that the mixture does not lose the nature of a liquid food. Hence, a small amount of cereal could be added to the milk, or some ground toast could be mixed with the broth. According to a preponderant number of the authors an egg-nog is sufficiently liquid in form to come under the heading of *"aliquid per modum potus"*.[394]

392 Vermeersch-Creusen, *Epitome Iuris Canonici*, II, 37; Cappello, *Tractatus Canonico-Moralis de Sacramentis*, I, 475.

393 Mahoney, "The Eucharistic Fast," *The Clergy Review*, IV (1932), 70.

394 S. C. S. Off., 7 sept. 1897—Fontes, n. 1192; cf. Vermeersch-Creusen, *Epitome Iuris Canonici*, II, 87; Prümmer, *Theologia Moralis*, III, 153.

Since the privilege of receiving Holy Communion is granted in this case in order that the sick may not be deprived of the Holy Eucharist for an extensive period of time, the Code conditions the use of the permission on the lack of any certain hope of a speedy convalescence. In the ordinary routine of affairs in daily life a "certain hope" may be regarded as at least the near equivalent of moral certainty. A recovery from one's sickness may be designated as "speedy" if a certified convalescence has appeared within three or four days.[395]

The Code does not specify that it must be impossible for the sick person to keep the fast. Can it be concluded, then, that this impossibility is not presupposed? Cappello and Vermeersch say that in virtue of canon 858, ¶2, the sick who have been confined to bed for a month and still furnish no assured hope of a speedy recovery may receive Holy Communion without fasting even though they were able to observe the fast.[396] Cappello argues that the Decree of 1906 made no mention of the fact whether or not the sick were able to observe the fast. Furthermore, he says that in the first two schemata of the Code that were drawn up it was expressly stated that the *sick who could keep the natural fast in its entirety* might receive once or twice a week, etc. Since these words were deleted in the text of the present Code, he concludes that this was done of set purpose, because the law giver did not wish to establish the sick person's inability to fast as one of the conditions for his reception of Holy Communion apart from the observance of the fast.

Such an interpretation seems to be too extensive if it be applied to all categories of the sick. It is more probable that only the sick who are habitually confined to bed have

395 Cappello, *Tractatus Canonico-Moralis de Sacramentis*, I, 475; Vermeersch-Creusen, *Epitome Iuris Canonici*, II, 87; "The Eucharistic Fast," *The Clergy Review*, XVI (1938), 253.

396 Vermeersch-Creusen, *loc. cit.;* Cappello, *Tractatus Canonici-Moralis de Sacramentis*, I, 470-474.

the privilege of receiving Communion without keeping the fast even if they are able to do so without injury to their health. However, since canon 858, ¶2, must be interpreted according to the old law which was contained in the Decree of 1906, and according to the authentic Declaration of the meaning of *infirmi* as given by the sacred Congregation of the Council in 1907, it is necessary to distinguish between those who are habitually confined to bed, and those who because of the nature of their illness cannot remain in bed, or who are able to be up for a few hours each day. The doubt proposed to the Sacred Congregation concerning the two latter classes specified that in the judgment of their physician they were not able to observe the natural fast. The same limitation, namely, the moral impossibility of keeping the fast, is implicitly contained in the Code. Hence, it would rather appear that in the case of those who are not able to remain in bed, or who are able to be out of bed for a few hours during the day, there must be a certain amount of difficulty for them to observe the Eucharistic fast before they can make use of the favor granted in canon 858, ¶2. It is not inconsistent to envisage the difficulty of keeping the fast as a condition which must be present for the one class of sick persons and not for the other, if the reception of Holy Communion without the observance of the fast is to be regarded as fully justified. The reason is that in the case of those who have been confined to bed for a month there is the presumption that they are seriously ill, and that there would be a probable danger in obliging them to observe the natural fast. For those who are not confined to bed there is a greater probability of self-deception in regard to their ability to keep the fast, and consequently a greater danger of abuse, if the question of the impossibility of keeping the fast were not left to the judgment of their physician.[397]

[397] Darmanin, "La Comunione Agli' Infermi non Digiuni," *Monitore Ecclesiastico*, 5 series, IV (1932), 132; Kinane, "Some Queries in Regard to the Modification of the Eucharistic Fast for the Sick," *IER*, XXV (1930), 520-521.

CHAPTER V

DISPENSATIONS FROM THE EUCHARISTIC FAST

The earliest known testimony of a dispensation which was granted from the observance of the Eucharistic fast was the concession which was given by Pope Julius III to the Emperor Charles V in 1554.[398] Subsequent to that time there are other examples of dispensation from the law of the fast, which were given in extraordinary cases, but only when some *causa publica* was the reason for the dispensation.[399]

In recent years, however, the need of a change in what is really but an ecclesiastical law became apparent. Rome, realizing this necessity of a change in the law of the Eucharistic fast, and ever ready to harmonize the laws of the Church with the actual needs of the faithful, is willing to grant dispensations from this law in favor of those who for some particular reason find it morally impossible to observe the natural fast.

The Sacred Congregation of the Holy Office is the competent authority to dispense priests from the Eucharistic fast which is required previous to the celebration of Holy Mass.[400] When a priest is under the necessity of saying a second Mass on the same day, or of saying Mass at a rather late hour, the Bishop may grant a dispensation from the Eucharistic fast, in urgent cases, in which there is not time

398 Benedictus XIV, ep. "*Quadam,*" 24 mart. 1756, ¶ 11, ¶ 12—Fontes, n. 439.

399 Benedictus XIV, *op. cit.*, ¶ 9, ¶ 13.

400 Canon 247, ¶ 5; cf. Litterae S. C. S. Off., Locorum Ordinariis Datae, Super Ieiunio Eucharistico Ante Missam—*AAS*, XV (1923), 151-152.

to have recourse to the Holy See. When necessity demands it, Rome is also willing to give local Ordinaries habitual faculties to dispense.[401]

The Sacred Congregation of the Sacraments grants the dispensation from the Eucharistic fast to the lay people, and to priests when they receive in the manner of the laity.[402] This same dispensation is granted to religious and to the members of those societies whose members live in common after the manner of religious, but who do not take vows, by the Sacred Congregation of Religious.

A Special Commission of Cardinals designated by the Holy Father in accordance with the ruling of canon 245 to settle a disputed question of competence as affecting two of the Roman Congregations, was asked: "Whether the power of granting to the religious of either sex a dispensation from the law of the Eucharistic fast for the receiving of Holy Communion belongs to the Sacred Congregation of the Sacraments, or to the Sacred Congregation of Religious." The reply was: "It belongs to the Sacred Congregation of Religious."[403] It is to be noted that this response has to do with the granting of a dispensation from the natural fast for the reception of Holy Communion, and not for the celebration of Holy Mass.

The Sacred Congregation for the Propagation of the Faith is the competent Congregation in the matter of the Eucharistic fast for those districts in which the hierarchy has not yet been established.[404] However, the Sacred Congregation of Religious grants this dispensation to religious of both sexes living in mission countries.[405]

The faithful of the Oriental Rite must petition the dis-

[401] S. C. S. Off., ep. 22 mart. 1923—*AAS*, XV (1923), 151.
[402] Canon 249, ¶ 1.
[403] Coetus, S. R. E. Cardinalium, 2 dec. 1922—*AAS*, XV (1923), 39; cf. also Bouscaren, *Canon Law Digest*, I, 162.
[404] Canon 252, ¶ 4.
[405] Cappello, *Tractatus Canonico-Moralis de Sacramentis*, I, 478.

pensation from the Eucharistic fast from the Sacred Congregation of the Oriental Church.[406] Nevertheless, the Sacred Congregation of the Holy Office is the authority competent to dispense priests of the Oriental Rite from the natural fast requisite for the celebration of Mass.[407]

In the formula of faculties which the Sacred Congregation for the Propagation of the Faith confers upon the Ordinaries in mission countries, there is contained the faculty of granting a dispensation from the Eucharistic fast to the sick for whom there is no hope of a speedy recovery. This dispensation can be given even before the end of a month's illness. The dispensation provides that medicine or liquid food may be taken by them before receiving Holy Communion. The laity may be permitted to receive Holy Communion without fasting two or three times a week. If there be question of priests or religious, the permission to receive Holy Communion daily while not fasting may be granted.[408]

Likewise, Nuncios and Internuncios for their jurisdictions, and Apostolic Delegates for the place of their mission, have the faculty of granting a dispensation to the sick who are confined to bed and concerning whom there is no certain hope of a speedy convalescence, by means of which dispensation the sick may receive Holy Communion after having taken medicine or liquid food previously, even in the case wherein their illness has not continued for as long as a month. They likewise have the faculty of granting this same permission before the expiration of a month to those, who are not confined to bed, but who are suffering from an illness of such a nature that they cannot keep the Eucharis-

406 Canon 257, ¶ 1.

407 Canon 257, ¶ 2.

408 Formulae Facultatum Quas S. C. De Prop. Fide Ordinariis in Terris Missionum Procurat, n. 17—Vermeersch-Creusen, *Epitome Iuris Canonici*, I, 642.

tic fast without injury to their health.[409]

Bishops cannot *iure proprio* grant a dispensation from the Eucharistic fast. They need an indult or a special faculty, which however, has been granted to many Bishops by the Holy See. In virtue of the ruling of canon 81 they may dispense from this law if there is difficulty in recourse to the Holy See, and at the same time, if there is present a danger of grave harm in delay. In the matter of the Eucharistic fast such a danger of serious harm is not frequent in view of the fact that canon 858, ¶1, allows those who are in danger of death to receive Holy Viaticum while not fasting, and ¶2 of the same canon makes like provision for all the sick whose malady consists of a month-long confinement which at the same time offers no certain hope of speedy convalescence.

The Holy Office, in a letter addressed to all local Ordinaries, announced that a partial mitigation of the Eucharistic fast may be obtained for priests in certain cases, and under certain conditions.[410] It is worthwhile to reproduce the letter in its entirety.

Suprema Sacra Congregatio S. Officii

Litterae, Locorum Ordinariis Datae, Super Ieiunio Eucharistico Ante Missam

Illme ac Revme Domine,

Optime novit Amplitudo Tua qua diligentissima cura legem ecclesiasticam ieiunii eucharistici, praesertim quod attinet ad sacerdotes sacrosanctum Missae sacrificium celebraturos, Sancta haec Apostolica Sedes semper tuita sit; nec dubitandum quin et in posterum eius observantia generatim urgeri debeat. Sed ne forte ex lege ecclesiastica qua reali Corpori Christi debitum praestatur obsequium, Corpus Christi mysticum seu animarum salus detrimentum capiat, Suprema haec Sacra Congregatio Sancti Officii, ex animo perpendens multitudinem officiorum quibus sacerdotes diebus festis incumbere debent ad commissum sibi gregem salutari pabulo enutriendum; et quod ob cleri penuriam multi ex eis Sanctae Missae

[409] Index Facultatum Quas, pro Locis Missionis suae, Nuntiis, internuntiis et Delegatis Apostolicis Penes Civitates seu Nationes, Post Codicis Iuris Canonici Publicationem Tribuere SSus Dominus Noster Decrevit, Ceteris Abrogatis, cap. IV, n. 42—Vermeersch-Creusen, *Eptiome Iuris Canonici*, I, 634.

[410] *AAS*, XV (1923), 151-152.

celebrationem iterare coguntur; idque non raro in locis longe dissitis, aditu difficilibus, inclementi aeris temperie divexatis, vel in aliis contrariis rerum et locorum adiunctis; decrevit in certis casibus et sub determinatis conditionibus eamdem ieiunii legem per opportunas dispensationes aliqua ex parte mitigare.

Quoties igitur sacerdotes, iuxta can 806, ¶2, Missam eodem die iterare aut etiam tardiore hora ad Sacrum Altare accedere necesse habeant; siquidem sine gravi damno ieiunii eucharistici legem, vel infirmae valetudinis causa, vel propter nimium sacri ministerii laborem, aliasve rationabiles causas, ad rigorem servare nequeant; Supremae huic Congregationi locorum Ordinarii, omnibus rerum adiunctis diligenter expositis, recurrere potuerunt. Quae pro diversitate casuum (sive cum singulis Ipsamet dispensando, sive, quando vera ac probata necessitas id omnino suadeat, habituales quoque facultates ipis Ordinariis tribuendo) opportune providebit. Quae quidem facultates pro casibus urgentioribus, in quibus tempus non per modum potus, exclusis inebriantibus, sumere permittatur; exercendae; hisce tamen sub conditionibus, ut nonnisi aliquid Quae conceduntur, per te ipsum graviter onerata conscientia, suppetat recurrendi ad S. Sedem iam ex nunc Amplitudini efficaciter scandalum removeatur; ac quamprimum S. Sedes de concessa dispensatione certior fiat.

Gravissime demum huius legis relaxationem solum concedendam esse scias, quum spirituale fidelium bonum id exigat, non vero obprivatam ipsius sacerdotis devotionem aut utilitatem.

Haec ad pastorale Tibi ministerium facilius utiliusque reddendum, probante SSmo. Domino Nostro Pio PP. XI, decreta, dum libens tecum communico fausta quoque ac felicia tibi adprecor a Domina.

Romae, ex aedibus Sancti Officii, 22 martii, 1923.

R. Card. Merry del Val Secretarius.

This letter of the Holy Office is addressed only to *Ordinarii locorum.* In accordance with the prescript of canon 198, ¶1, the following are *Ordinarii locorum*: the residential Bishop, the abbot and the prelate nullius, and their vicar general, the administrator, the vicar and the prefect apostolic, and those who in case of the vacancy of the above offices succeed to the office by the provisions of law. Major superiors of exempt religious orders are not included in the term *"Ordinarii locorum."*[411] Hence they cannot dispense their subjects from the law of the Eucharistic fast in virtue of this letter.

The faculty which is delegated to Ordinaries to dispense

[411] Canon 198, ¶2.

their priests from the Eucharistic fast in urgent cases is to be exercised by the Ordinaries themselves, so that it may not be further delegated. Vermeersch, commenting on this letter of the Holy Office, says that the Bishop cannot subdelegate this power to his vicar general.[412] Contrary to this opinion, it appears that no delegation on the part of the Bishop is necessary in order that the vicar general may exercise this faculty of dispensing priests from the Eucharistic fast in urgent cases, since this faculty is granted in a general manner to all local Ordinaries by the Holy Office itself. In accordance with canon 198, ¶1, the vicar general is a local Ordinary and therefore comes under the provision which is made by the letter of the Holy Office for all local Ordinaries to dispense their priests from the Eucharistic fast when there is not time to have recourse to the Holy See. Moreover, since the delegation to dispense priests from the Eucharistic fast under the conditions enumerated in the letter of the Holy Office is not given to the Bishop *intuitu personae,* but *ratione officii,* the exercise of this faculty should not be restricted in such a manner that the Bishop only may make use of it, to the exclusion of the vicar general.

In its introductory part the letter first of all directs attention to the diligent care with which the Holy See has always maintained the law of the Eucharistic fast, and insists on the fact that its observance will continue to be urged in the future. Lest, however, so the letter continues, the reverence thus shown to the real Body of Christ in the Blessed Sacrament should prove a detriment to His Mystical Body, the Sacred Congregation, taking into consideration the numerous duties of priests on days of precept, and taking into consideration the fact that because of the scarcity of priests it is oftentimes necessary for priests to say two Masses in places far apart, in places difficult to reach, under conditions of inclement weather or under other un-

[412] "Ieiunium ante Missam," *Periodica,* XII (1923), 32.

favorable circumstances, has deemed it advisable to mitigate somewhat this law of the fast by suitable dispensations. Thus the principle underlying the granting of this relaxation is that the dispensation is meant chiefly for the benefit of the faithful. Accordingly the priest may not make use of it for his own private devotion or utility.

The letter then goes on to say that whenever, in accordance with canon 806, ¶2, priests find it necessary to say two Masses on the same day, or even to say one Mass at a rather late hour, if they cannot, without grave inconvenience, observe the natural fast, because of infirm health, or because of the heavy labors of the ministry, or other reasonable causes, the local Ordinaries may have recourse to the Holy Office, which alone is competent in all matters relating to the Eucharistic fast incumbent on priests for the celebration of Mass, and which will then make suitable provisions for the various cases, or, when real necessity demands it, will give the local Ordinaries themselves habitual faculties to dispense.

According to the prescript of canon 806, ¶2, bination is permitted only on days of precept. However, the Masses at a late hour may be necessary on ferial days also. In the case of bination it is not necessary that the second Mass should be at a late hour. This is specified only for the case in which but one Mass is said. The Sacred Congregation did not define what it considered as a late hour. Much will depend on the circumstances in particular cases. Eleven o'clock would certainly be a late hour, while any time before ten o'clock can hardly be considered a late hour.[413] Eventual serious injury to the priest's health constitutes the requisite condition for the dispensation. The observance of the Eucharistic fast in all its rigor may result in this serious injury either on account of the celebrant's weak

[413] MacCarthy, "The Eucharistic Fast," *ER*, LXIX (1923), 186; Vermeersch, *Theologica Moralis*, III, 252; "Notes and Queries," *IER*, XXI (1923), 524.

health, or because of the work of his ministry which is so heavy that it imposes on him a great strain, *e.g.*, bination in widely separated places, together with the distribution of Holy Communion and the preaching of a sermon in both Masses, and possibly the hearing of confessions or the holding of a catechism class for the children between Masses.

The normal procedure in seeking this dispensation is to have the local Ordinary of the priest concerned apply to the Holy Office, laying all the circumstances of the case before the Sacred Congregation. The normal case is that in which there is time to have recourse to the Holy See. In those dioceses wherein there is frequent need for this dispensation the Ordinaries may apply for habitual faculties to dispense their priests from the Eucharistic fast.

In more urgent cases the local Ordinary himself may dispense. An urgent case is one in which one cannot await the time necessary for an exchange of correspondence between the diocese and the Holy Office. This urgency is a matter of relativity, and differs according to distance. It is left to the prudence of the Ordinary to judge of the urgency of the case. For these urgent cases the Ordinary does not have to presume permission in order to grant this concession. The faculty to dispense priests from the Eucharistic fast in urgent cases in conceded to him by the Holy Office. However, it must be exercised personally by the local Ordinary himself, and cannot be further delegated.

When an Ordinary dispenses in a case of urgency he does so with a conscience gravely burdened with responsibility. He must proceed only when there is a verification of the following conditions: 1) That only something by way of drink and exclusive of alcoholic beverages be permitted. Hence, solid food of whatever nature, even when taken as medicine, may not be allowed; 2) That scandal must be efficaciously precluded. Scandal here is to be understood as the offense of the pious. This can be effectively guarded against by prescribing that the nourishment is to be taken privately. If this is not possible, then the faithful should in some manner be informed of the fact that a special dispensation has been granted to the priest for good reasons. This notice, of course, is served with a view to exercising all needed precaution against the possible disedification of the faithful; 3) That the Holy See be informed of the granted dispensation as soon as possible. This obligation which the Holy Office imposes on Ordinaries to make an early report constitutes a serious duty.[414]

Priests who are dispensed from the Eucharistic fast before the second Mass may take the ablutions at the first Mass.[415] Since the Holy Office has declared that priests who are dispensed from the Eucharistic fast may take the ablutions in their first Mass, it seems that they should do so in accordance with the prescripts of the Rubrics of the Missal, unless there is present a danger of scandal, *v.g.*, persons seeing the priest take the ablutions, and who not knowing that he enjoys a dispensation from the Eucharistic fast, might think that the priest is committing a sin by breaking his fast.

The same Congregation of the Holy Office, on July 1, 1931, issued a more closely determined list of norms to serve as a guide in applying for this indult.[416] The points

414 Vermeersch, "Dispensatio a Ieiunio Eucharistico ante Celebrationem," *Periodica*, XII (1923), 32; Villien, "La Dispense du Jeûne Eucharistique pour les Prêtres," *Le Canoniste Contemporain*, XLVI (1924), 14; "Notes and Queries," *IER*, XXI (1923), 526.

415 S. C. S. Off., "Declaratio circa Dispensationem a Lege Ieiunii Eucharistici circa Missam"—*AAS*, XV (1923), 585.

416 S. C. S. Off., Normae 1 iulii 1931, A Locorum Ordinariis Prae Oculis Habendae in Petendis Dispensationibus a Lege Ieiunii Eucharistici Pro Sacerdotibus Ante Missae Celebrationem:

1. Dispensatio a lege ieiunii eucharistici concedi potest ad aliquid sumendum sive per modum potus ad vires physicas reficiendas et sustinendas sive per modum verae medicinae ad morborum effectibus occurrendum.

2. Cum ratio dispensationis per modum potus publicum sit bonum spirituale fidelium, ab iis tantummodo sacerdotibus impetrari potest, qui animarum curae sunt addicti; dispensatio per modum verae medicinae, cum in commodum etiam privatum sit inducta, ceteris quoque sacerdotibus potest concedi, prima pro diebus tantum festivis vel

to be included in the petition for the dispensation from the Eucharistic fast for priests are: the age and the ecclesiastical office of the priest, the fact whether he is charged with the care of souls, a medical certificate concerning his state of health, testifying to the necessity that he take medicine or liquid food before Mass, stating specifically what liquid food or medicine is intended, the hour of celebration, and any other circumstances in the case of binating, along with

ferialibus conceditur, in quibus missa sacrificium hora tardiore (post horam decimam) ratione ministerii est celebrandum; altera etiam pro omnibus diebus.

3. Dispensatio huiusmodi, cum sit gravis relaxatio legis ecclesiasticae, gravem, ut patet requirit causam, quae in singulis casibus est comprobanda; unde fit ut dispensatio nunquam indiscriminatim sacerdotibus indeterminatis, sed semper singulis tantum sacerdotibus determinatis concedatur, singulorum personalibus adiunctis rite perpensis.

4. In relativo supplici libello S. Congregationi exhibendo sequentia sunt indicanda:

a) oratoris aetas:
b) eius officium vel munus, seu an ipse qua parochus vel saltem qua vicarius paroecialis (can. 451-478) curae animarum operam det;
c) eius valetundinis status per medici testimonium comprobatus, ex quo una cum morbo appareat etiam an ipse aliquid per modum potus vel per modum medicinae sumere debeat et in utroque casu de quonam potu vel de quanam medicina specifice agatur;
d) utrum unam an duas missas diebus dominicis et festis ipse celebret; quanam hora et, si bis celebret, ubinam celebret, utrum scilicet in eadem ecclesia, an vero in diversis ecclesiis, indicata in casu earum ad invicem distantia, praesertim si iter pedibus sit peragendum;
e) an ab alio sacerdote firmioris valetudinis possit substitui.

Quae omnia indicanda sunt prima vice qua dispensatio imploratur, dum pro gratiae iam semel impetratae prorogatione non requiruntur, si eaedem oratoris circumstantiae iam expositae adhuc perdurent.

5) Supplex libellus sacerdotum saecularium ab ipso Episcopo, addito suo voto, est subsignandus; libelus supplex religiosorum, qui animarum curae operam dant, tum ab Episcopo loci, ubi eorum domus religiosa est constituta, tum ab ipso suo Superiore Generali; supplex libellus religiosorum, qui curam animarum non exercent, tantum et exclusive a suo Superiore Generali.

6) In prorogatione imploranda aut praecedens rescriptum exhibeatur, aut saltem eiusdem rescripti numerus indicetur.

Romae, ex aedibus S. Officii, die iulii 1931.

Angelus Subrizi, Supremae S. Congr. S. Officii Notarius. cf. Vermeersch, "Dispensatio a Ieiunio Eucharistico ante Celebrationem," Periodica, XXI (1932), 105-108.

information concerning the possibility of getting another priest to do the work of the petitioner.

In the case of secular priests the petition is to be signed by the Bishop and accompanied with his *votum.* In the case of religious who have the care of souls the intervention of the Superior General is also required. For religious who have not the care of souls the petition for the dispensation is to be signed solely and exclusively by the Superior General.

A comparison of this list of rules with the previous letter "*Optime novit*" of the Holy Office reveals an important distinction between the two documents. According to the terms of the "*Optime novit,*" the dispensation from the Eucharistic fast was granted only for the spiritual welfare of the faithful, and not for the sake of the private devotion or advantage of the priest. The norms to be followed in seeking a dispensation from the Eucharistic fast for priests, as given by the Holy Office in 1931 distinguish between the case in which a dispensation is asked for the priest to take something "*per modum potus ad vires reficiendas*" and the case in which a dispensation is requested to take something "*per modum verae medicinae ad morborum effectibus occurrendum*". This distinction makes the conditions on which an indult may be obtained much less strict for those cases in which a dispensation is requested to take medicine only, but not liquid food before the celebration of Holy Mass. A dispensation to take medicine before the celebration of Mass is not limited to cases where a relaxation of the law is desirable for the spiritual good of the faithful, but may be permitted for the private advantages of the priest. In this latter case the use of the priest's privilege of saying Mass while not fasting is not limited to days of precept, or to those occasions when it is necessary for the priest to say a late Mass, but may be used on ferial days, and even though the Mass is not necessarily at a late hour. However, when a dispensation is petitioned for in the private utility of the priest, the practice of the Sacred Congregation of the Holy Office is to permit only the use of medicine, and not any other liquid or solid food.[417]

Faculties for the laity are also granted by the Holy See. Local Ordinaries in many places have obtained from the Sacred Congregation of the Sacraments a triennial faculty, which they may subdelegate to certain priests or to all within their jurisdiction, by which the terms of canon 858, ¶2, are considerably extended as to persons entitled to the privilege. All persons who have completed their fifty-ninth year, pregnant mothers and those suckling their infants, may communicate, even daily, after breaking the fast by taking medicine or liquid nourishment.[418]

The Sacred Congregation of the Sacraments has also been known to grant general faculties to bishops, whereby they may give dispensations to all the faithful who are confined by sickness to hospitals and clinics, and who because of their illness cannot observe the natural fast, even before the expiration of a month. Similar indults have been obtained by bishops to dispense those in convalescent homes and homes for the aged.[419]

[417] Vermeersch, "Dispensatio a Ieiunio Eucharistico ante Missae Celebrationem," *Periodica*, XXI (1932), 107; "Eucharistic Fast," *Clergy Review*, XV (1938), 169.

[418] *Nederlandsche Katholiske Stemmen*, XXXVI (1936), 381—cited by the author of "The Eucharistic Fast," *Clergy Review*, XIII (1937), 227. Here is the text of such an Indult obtained by the Archbishop of Malines, December 15, 1936: "Sacra Congregatio de Disciplina Sacramentorum, vigore specialium facultatum sibi a SSmo Domino Nostro Pio XI tributarum, attentis expositis ab SSmo Ordinario Mechliensi, Eidem tribuit facultates iuxta petitas, ad triennium, ut tum in sexagesimo anno constitutis et adversa valetudine laborantibus, tum mulieribus pregnantibus, tum aegrotis in nosocomiis degentibus veniam largiatur aliquid sumendi per modum potus vel medicinae ante SS. Eucharistiae Communionem, bis vel ter in hebdomada de consilio confessariorum durante male affecta valetudine, praegnatione et commoratione in nosocomio, remota quacumque scandali et admirationis occasione. Contrariis quibuscumque minime obstantibus. D. Card. Jorio, *Praef.*—cf. Clergy Review, *loc. cit.*

[419] Jorio, *La Comunione Agl' Infermi*, p. 34.

If permission to take solid food is desired, it seems that it will not easily be obtained. Jorio mentions one case where permission to take solid food before the reception of Holy Communion was granted. He also mentions another case where it was refused.[420]

The petition for a dispensation from the Eucharistic fast should be addressed to the Ordinary, stating exactly what is requested, and it should be accompanied by a medical certificate. The Ordinary will then under his signature forward it to the respective Congregation.

In 1927, in view of the peculiar and extraordinary circumstances then existing in Mexico, the Holy Father granted to the people of Mexico a dispensation whereby they could receive the most Blessed Eucharist at any hour of the day or night, even without fasting. However, if they were able to foresee the time of Communion, they were to fast for one hour before receiving.[421]

In 1929 an Indult of the Commission for Russia under date of November 25, 1929, authorized Bishops and Administrators Apostolic in Russia to permit the celebration of Mass and the reception of Holy Communion in the afternoon or evening, on condition that a Eucharistic fast of four hours was observed.[422]

A private indult of the Sacred Congregation of the Sacraments, March 29, 1926, granted to the members of the Association of Priest Adorers of the Blessed Sacrament, for seven years, the privilege during illness of receiving Communion without observing the strict Eucharistic fast, under certain conditions, one of which was that the per-

420 Jorio, *loc. cit.*

421 Extraordinary Faculties Granted to Ordinaries and People of Mexico (S. C. Conc., 23 dec. 1927) Private—Bouscaren, *Canon Law Digest, Supplement*—1938, p. 3.

422 Mass and Communion in Evening (Commission for Russia, Indult, 25 nov. 1929) Private—Bouscaren, *Canon Law Digest*, II, 87.

mission of the Ordinary of the place was previously obtained.[423]

In an Apostolic Letter of March 7, 1924, His Holiness, Pius XI, after reviewing the history and spiritual advantages of Eucharistic Congresses, declared certain indulgences, privileges, and dispensations in favor of those participating in them. If there is public adoration of the Blessed Sacrament all night during any Eucharistic Congress, one Mass may be said at midnight, at which Holy Communion may be distributed. Priests who have been present may, at the conclusion of this midnight Mass, or at 1 A.M., celebrate Mass.[424]

In this indult, unlike most of the other privileges in regard to the celebration of Holy Mass or the reception of Holy Communion at an unusual hour and in exceptional circumstances, no period of fasting was prescribed as a condition for the use of the dispensation.

The official ecclesiastical organ of the diocese of Muenster, August 5, 1938, has the following notice:

By virtue of the authority granted me by the Sacred Congregation of the Sacraments, I give permission for those employed in mines and as coke burners and for all laborers living in the diocese of Muenster who regularly throughout the year work at night, to receive Holy Communion once a month with the advice of their confessor, even though they may have taken some liquid food beforehand.

The use of the privilege, however, is not allowed in those months of the year in which a worker by way of exception has one or more days free from night work.

[423] Eucharistic Fast: Privilege of Members of the Association of Priest Adorers of the Blessed Sacrament (S. C. Sacr.) Private—Bouscaren, *Canon Law Digest*, I, 409.

[424] "Indulgentiae, Privilegia, Indulta et Dispensationes Conceduntur Iis Qui Conventibus Eucharisticis Celebrandis Intersint vel Operam Navent"—*AAS*, XVI (1924), 156.

The confessors are admonished, before they give their consent for the workers to receive Holy Communion while not fasting, to instruct them as to the conditions and limits of the privilege and to take care to remove all danger of scandal and moral bewilderment.

Muenster, 27 juli 1938. Der Bischop von Muenster: Clemens August.[425]

The formula for petitioning a dispensation from the Eucharistic fast is as follows: "Beatissime Pater, N.N., Diocesis N.N., quamvis non decumbat propter infirmitatem, attamen tanta stomachi debilitate laborat, ut ei moraliter impossibile sit observare ieiunium naturale ante s. communionem praescriptum. Ideo ad Sanctitatis Vestrae pedes humiliter provolutus, suppliciter petit facultatem sumendi aliquid per modum potus [vel per modum medicinae, vel per modum cibi solidi] antequam ad s. communionem recipiendam accedat."[426]

425 (Ieiunium eucharisticum—Erleichterung.) DasKirchliche Amtsblatt für die Diozese Munster, Nr. 17, vom 5. August 1938 enthalt folgende Bekannt-machung:

Es ist hier folgendes Reskript der S. Congregatio de disciplina Sacramentorum vom 24 Mai d. J. eingegangen:

Num. 2177/38.

Beatissime Pater,

Episcopus Monasterien., ad pedes S. V. provolutus, humiliter postulat facultatem permittendi operariis metallis addictis, qui operas fabriles in officina praebent per totum annum, nocturno tempore, ut semel in mense aliquid per modum potus sumere possint ante Sanctissimam Eucharisticam Communionem.

Ex Audientia Ssmi diei 24 Maii 1938.

Sanctissimus Dominus Noster Pius Papa XI, audita relatione infrascripti Card. Praefecti Sacrae Congregationis de Sacramentis, attentis expositis, Episcopo Monasterien. facultatem tribuere dignatus est iuxta petita, ad triennium ut praefatis fidelibus veniam largiatur aliquid sumendi per modum potus semel in mense de consilio confessariorum, ante Ssmam Eucharisticam Communionem, remoto quocumque scandalo et periculo admirationis. Contrariis quibuscumque non obstantibus.

sign. D. Card. Jorio Praef.
csign. F. Bracci Secr. cf. *Theologisch-praktische Quartalschrift*, XCII (1939), 139-140.

426 Noldin, *Theologia Moralis*, III, 175.

A doctor's certificate testifying to the fact that the person is unable to observe the natural fast should accompany this petition. If the dispensation is asked for a lay person the petition should be addressed to the Sacred Congregation of the Sacraments; if for a religious, to the Sacred Congregation of Religious. The dispensation for a priest to celebrate Mass without observing the Eucharistic fast is to be addressed to the Sacred Congregation of the Holy Office, and must be accompanied by the necessary information which the Holy Office demands. All petitions are ordinarily to be sent to the respective Congregations through the local Ordinary.

CHAPTER VI

PENALTIES AGAINST PRIESTS WHO VIOLATE THE EUCHARISTIC FAST

Before the Code there was no penalty determined by general legislation against priests who celebrated Holy Mass after having broken the natural fast. Several sanctions were attached to this violation by particular Councils in an attempt to root out abuses in this matter. For example, the III Council of Braga (572) ruled that any priest who was found guilty of violating the precept of the Eucharistic fast was to be deprived of his office and deposed by his bishop.[427] The VII Council of Toledo (646) inflicted the penalty of excommunication,[428] and the II Council of Macon (585) punished priests who were delinquent in the law of the Eucharistic fast with the loss of any dignity or honor they held.[429]

The Code does away with these arbitrary punishments. Canon 2321, states: "Priests, who in violation of canon 808, presume to celebrate Mass after having broken the natural fast, shall be suspended from the celebration of Mass for a period of time to be fixed by the Ordinary in proportion to the special circumstances of the case."

This punishment is not incurred *ipso facto,* but must be inflicted by the Ordinary when the law has evidently been *violated.* In other words, it is *suspensio ferendae sententiae* and not *latae sententiae.*

[427] C. 10—Mansi, IX, 841.
[428] C. 2—Mansi, X, 767.
[429] C. 6—Mansi, IX, 952.

It is worthy of notice that the sanction of this penal law assumes the note of presumption to be attached to the actual transgression. To *presume* is to dare, to attempt something contrary to the law, and implies knowledge and malice. Hence, only those who knowingly and willingly violate the prescript of canon 808, are liable to incur the penalty of suspension, stated in canon 2321. By analogy canon 2229, ¶2, which deals with *latae sententiae* penalties, may be applied here.[430] Any reason, therefore, of (not affected) ignorance, or fear, or physical incapacity would diminish imputability. But since the penalty is not a *latae sententiae* penalty these reasons do not entirely exempt one from incurring it. However, since the text expressly adds the term *praesumpserit,* it evidently admits a diminution of imputability and implies that the transgression must be a rash one.[431] Thus, a priest who believes that he has a reason—although in the case this reason be actually insufficient in itself—for saying Mass after having broken the Eucharistic fast is not comprehended under this law, since it has in view only a fully deliberate offense which entails a disregard and contempt for the prescription of the Church.[432]

Woywod says that the local Ordinary has the right to judge if there was sufficient excuse to warrant the celebration of Mass after the fast was broken, and if he does not take the same view of the excuses as the priest, but penalizes him for saying Mass after the breaking of the fast, the priest is obliged to submit to the penalty.[433]

The threat of this penalty is enunciated in the law *verbis prœceptivis,* and therefore it must ordinarily be inflicted as often as there is evidence of a violation of the law. The

[430] "Si lex habeat verba: praesumpserit, . . .aliave similia quae plenam cognitionem ac deliberationem exigunt, quaelibet imputabilitatis imminutio sive ex parte intellectus sive ex parte voluntatis eximit a poenis latae sententiae."

[431] Augustine, *A Commentary on Canon Law,* VIII, 304.

[432] Ayrinhac-Lydon, *Penal Legislation in the New Code of Canon Law* (New York: Benziger Brothers, 1936), p. 174.

[433] *A Practical Commentary on the Code of Canon Law,* II, 474.

specified duration of the suspension is for its determination left to the judgment of the Ordinary, who, taking into account the aggravating or extenuating circumstances, will proportion the punishment to the moral and judicial contingencies of the offense. These circumstances may be extremely serious in character on account of the ensuing scandal or in view of bad example they entail, *e.g.*, if intemperance was the reason for the violation. However, they may be less serious in view of the fact that they are occasioned by the local need of priests or other similar conditions.[434]

Suspension, even though it be temporary, belongs to the class of *vindictive* penalties[435] and consequently requires a judiciary procedure for its infliction, if proof in court is needed to establish the certainty of the delict's commission. While it thus ordinarily requires a judiciary process, the case may nevertheless furnish a reason for suspension *per modum praecepti* and even *ex informata conscientia,* if the Ordinary cannot proceed in the judiciary way, without grave inconvenience.[436]

Moreover, in order to proceed with a suspension *ex informata conscientia,* it is necessary that in accordance with canon 2191, ¶1, the delict be occult, or according to canon 2191, ¶2, if it is public, that one of the following circumstances be present:

1) If conscientious and responsible witnesses make the offense known to the Ordinary, but cannot in any way be induced to testify in court to the crime, and there are no

434 Canon 2223, ¶ 3: "Si vero lex utatur verbis praeceptivis, ordinarie poena infligenda est."; Blat, *Commentarium Codicis* (6 vols., Romae: 1921-1924), I, 121; Augustine, *A Commentary on Canon Law,* VIII, 305.

435 Canon 2298, n. 2.

436 Canon 1933, ¶ 4: "Poenitentia, . . .suspenio, . . .dummodo delictum certum est, infligi possunt etiam per modum praecepti extra iudicium."; Canon 2186, ¶ 1: "Ordinariis licet ex informata conscientia clericos suos subditos suspendere ab officio sive ex parte sive etiam in totum."; Canon 2186, ¶ 2: "Extraordinarium hoc remedium adhibere non licet, si Ordinarius potest sine gravi incommodo ad juris normam in subditum procedere."

other proofs available by which it can be proved in a judicial trial;

2) If the cleric himself by threats or by the use of other means prevents the institution of a judicial trial against himself, or hinders the completion of a trial already commenced;

3) If hindrances to the conduct of a judicial trial and to the final rendering of a judicial sentence arise from adverse civil laws or from a serious danger of eventual scandal.[437]

Canon 2197 states that an offense is occult when it is not public. The same canon explains that an offense is public when a knowledge of it has been divulged to two or more persons, or if the circumstances of the offense are such that it can and must be prudently foreseen that the offense will easily come to the knowledge of the public. If only a few persons know of the offense, and it is likely that they will not reveal it, it is still occult.

However, since suspension *ex informata conscientia* is an extraordinary remedy, the Ordinary should not make use of the power of inflicting this penalty in this extrajudicial manner when he can proceed in the judiciary way without great inconvenience.[438] Hence, even if there are only a few persons who have direct knowledge of the offense, yet the offense can be proved against the priest, then the Ordinary is not to proceed with the offense *ex informata conscientia,* for in such a case he can without great inconvenience proceed against him by ordinary trial.

Suspension *ex informata conscientia* can never be inflicted for a notorious crime, because such a crime requires judiciary procedure, in order to safeguard the public welfare and the authority of the law.[439]

[437] Augustine, *A Commentary on Canon Law,* VII, 480-481.
[438] Canon 2186, ¶ 2.
[439] Canon 2191, ¶ 2; Augustine, *A Commentary on Canon Law,* VII, 480.

Canon 2190, is to be strictly observed in regard to investigation and proofs if the suspension is to be inflicted *ex informata conscientia.*[440] Formerly if the suspension *ex informata conscientia,* was inflicted for an indefinite length of time the duration of the penalty was considered to be perpetual, and the infliction of a perpetual suspension *ex informata conscientia* was in turn held to be invalid.[441] The Code, however, does not make a perpetual suspension of this kind invalid, yet it cautions the Ordinary to abstain from inflicting this penalty *in perpetuum.*[442] The decree of suspension *ex informata conscientia* ordinarily is to be given in writing and should designate the day, month, and year of the decree. It is to be expressly stated that the suspension is inflicted for reasons known to the Ordinary, and it should indicate the duration of the suspension.[443] It is left to the prudent judgment of the Ordinary to disclose or conceal from the priest the reason for the suspension *ex informata conscientia.*[444]

A suspension which is inflicted as a vindictive penalty for a determined length of time ceases *ipso facto* when the period of time for which it was inflicted expires. An illicit violation of the suspension does not interrupt, nor does it prolong the period of time of the suspension.[445] Before the time for the duration of which the penalty was inflicted expires, the suspension may be remitted by dispensation in accordance with the prescript of canon 2236.[436] A sus-

[440] "Ordinarius, qui fert suspensionem ex informata conscientia, debet ex peractis investigationibus tales collegisse probationes, quae eum certum reddant clericum delictum revera perpetrasse et quidem adeo grave ut eiusmodi poena coercendus sit."

[441] S. C. C., 20 dec. 1873—*ASS,* VII (1872), 569-575.

[442] Canon 2188, n. 2; Woywod, *A Practical Commentary on the Code of Canon Law,* II, 399.

[443] Canon 2188, nn. 1, 2, 3.

[444] Canon 2193.

[445] Canon 2289; Cappello, *De Censuris* (3 ed., Romae: Marietti, 1933), p. 441.

[446] Canon 2289; Canon 2236, ¶ 1: "Remissio poenae. . .per dispensationem, si agatur de poenis vindicativis, concedi tantum potest ab eo qui poenam tulit, vel ab eius competente Superiore aut successore, vel ab eo cui haec potestas commissa est."

pension which is inflicted *ad beneplacitum superioris* can not be taken away except by dispensation. However, it ceases with the death or removal of the Ordinary who issued the sentence.[447]

The Code speaks of Ordinaries in general in canon 2321, and in the canons which treat of suspension *ex informata conscientia*. Included under the term "Ordinary" are the following: the residential bishop, the abbot and prelate *nullius*, the administrator, the vicar and prefect apostolic. However, the vicar-general is excluded, unless he has obtained a special commission from his bishop. Furthermore, those persons are Ordinaries who in the case of vacancy of the above offices succeed to the office by the provisions of law. In exempt clerical religious organization the major superiors are Ordinaries over their subjects. They have the same jurisdiction over their subjects that the local Ordinary has over the secular priests of his diocese.[448]

A suspension which is inflicted by judicial sentence takes effect as soon as the sentence is pronounced, and an appeal *in devolutivo* only is granted.[449] Appeal is defined in canon 1879, as implying the right of turning from an inferior superior who pronounced the sentence for the sake of obtaining redress before a higher judge. The distinction between an appeal *in suspensivo* and an appeal *in devolutivo* is explained by canon 1889. An appeal *in suspensivo* suspends the execution of the appealed sentence. An appeal *in devolutivo* does not suspend the sentence, even though the merit of the case is still pending by reason of the appeal.

From a suspension *ex informata conscientia* there is no appeal to the Metropolitan or to a court of second instance.

[447] S. C. de Prop. Fide, instr. 20 oct 1884, n. 6—Collectanea S. Congregationis de Propaganda Fide, n. 1628; cf. Wernz-Vidal, Jus Canonicum (Vol. VI, Pars secunda, Romae: apud Aedes Universitatis Gregorianae, 1928), 765.

[448] Canon 198, ¶ 1.

[449] Canon 2243, ¶ 1.

It is a general principle in law that from the disciplinary and administrative acts of the Ordinary there is no appeal, but only from judicial sentence, and suspension *ex informata conscientia* is not a judicial proceeding. However, the suspended priest may have recourse to the Holy See. This recourse is *in devolutivo* only, and the priest in the meantime must abstain from the acts which are forbidden him by the suspension. An instruction of the Sacred Congregation of the Propagation of the Faith explicitly stated that the recourse to the Holy See did not relieve anyone from complying with the effects of the suspension until the Holy See has rendered a contrary decision.[450]

If the cleric has recourse to the Holy See against the suspension *ex informata conscientia*, the Ordinary must forward to the Holy See the proofs by which it is established that the priest actually committed an offense which may be punished with this extraordinary penalty.[451]

[450] S. C. de Prop. Fide, instr. 20 oct. 1884,—*Collectanea S. Congregationis de Propaganda Fide*, n. 1628; Woywod, *A Practical Commentary on the Code of Canon Law*, II, 406.

[451] Canon 2194.

CONCLUSIONS

A study of the law of the Eucharistic fast has led to the following conclusions:

1. The law of the Eucharistic fast, while a purely ecclesiastical law, obliges with a severity unknown in any other purely ecclesiastical discipline, not involving validity.

2. However, a marked contrast is manifest in the attitude which the Church has manifested in recent years in regard to the discipline of the natural fast enjoined before the reception of Holy Communion, and more especially in regard to the prescript which requires that the priest be fasting for the celebration of Holy Mass.

3. The rules of canon 33 in regard to the choice of the various reckonings of time may be applied in the observance of the law of the Eucharistic fast, so that one may make use of any of the various computations of time in reckoning the hour of midnight. This liberty or choice of making use of any of the various manners of reckoning time is not limited in such a manner, that having chosen one computation of time for a certain precept, we are bound to follow the same computation for all other precepts which oblige simultaneously or consecutively. One may make use simultaneously of a double choice of times in regard to the observance of two formally distinct precepts.

4. The privilege of receiving Holy Communion while not fasting which is granted to the sick by canon 858, ¶2, is to be interpreted in a wide sense. The extensive interpretation which was given by the Sacred Congregation of the Council to the term "*decumbentes*" may be

applied to the words "*qui decumbunt*" of canon 858, ¶2. The month of which it is question in canon 858, ¶2, may be reckoned morally, i.e., as a period of twenty-six or twenty-seven days.

5. Those who are not included in the term "*decumbentes*" as it is used in canon 858, ¶2, but who find it morally impossible to observe the natural fast, may petition a dispensation, and be fairly well assured that they will obtain it, if their case warrants the granting of a dispensation.

6. The penalty of suspension from the celebration of Mass which is stated *verbis praeceptivis* in canon 2321 is a *ferendae sententiae* penalty. Since it belongs to the class of vindictive penalties it requires a judiciary process. However, it may form a reason for suspension *per modum praecepti* or *ex informata conscientia.* In either case an appeal from the sentence is *in devolutivo* only.

BIBLIOGRAPHY

SOURCES

Acta Apostolicae Sedis, Commentarium Officiale, Romae, 1909—
Acta et Decreta Sacrorum Conciliorum Recentiorum Collectio Lacensis, Auctoribus Presbyteris S. J. e domo B. V. M. Sine Labe Conceptae ad Lacum, 7 vols., Friburgi Brisgoviae, 1870-1890.
Acta Sanctae Sedis, 41 vols., Romae, 1865-1908.
Bullarium SSmi Domini Nostri Benedicti Papae XVI, 4 ed., 4 vols., Venetiis, 1778.
Caeremoniale Episcoporum, iussu editum Benedicti XIV et Leonis XIII, Mechlinae: Dessain, 1887.
Canones et Decreta Sacrosancti Oecumenici Concilii Tridentini, Roma: Ex typo. polyglotta S. C. de Propaganda Fide, 1904.
Catechismus ex Decreto Concilii Tridentini ad Parochoa Pii Quinti Pont. Max. et deinde Clementis XIII, iussu editum Taurinae, 1896.
Codex Iuris Canonici Pii Pontificis Maximi iuusu digestus, Benedicti Papae XV auctoritate promulgatus, Romae: Typis Polyglottis Vaticanis, 1917.
Codicis Iuris Canonici Fontes cura Emi Petri Card. Gasparri editi (Vols. VII-IX *editi cura et studio Emi Justiniani Card. Seredi*), 9 vols., Romae: Typis Polyglottis Vaticanis, 1923-1939.
Collectanea S. Congregationis de Propaganda Fide, 2 vols., Romae: Typographis Polyglotta S. C. de Propaganda Fide, 1907.
Corporis Iuris Canonici, editio Lipsiensis 2, post Aemilii Ludovici Richteri curas ad Librorum Manu Scriptorum et Editionis Romanae Fidem Recognovit et Adnotatione Critica Instruxit Aemilius Friedberg, 2 vols., Lipsiae, 1879-1881.
Decretales D. Gregorii Papae IX, Suae Interpretati una cum Glossis Restitutae, Romae: In aedibus Populi Romani, 1632.
Harduin, *Acta Conciliorum et Epistolae Decretales ac Constitutiones Summorum Pontificum*, 12 vols., Parisiis, 1715.
Mansi, *Sacrorum Conciliorum Nova et Amplissima Collectio*, 58 vols., Paris-Leipzig-Arnhem, 1901-1927.
Missale Romanum ex Decreto Sacrosancti Consilii Tridentini Restitutum, S. Pii V Pontificio Maximi, iussu editum. Aliorum Pontificum cura Recognitum a Pio X Reformatum et SSmi D. N. Benedicti XV, auctoritate vulgatum, Ratisbone: Sumptibus et Typis Friderici Pustet, 1925.
Pitra, *Iuris Ecclesiastici Graecorum Historia et Monumenta, Iussu Pii IX, Pont. Max. Curante*, 2 vols., Vol. I, a Primo P. C. N. ad VI Saeculum, Romae, 1864.
Rituale Romanum, Pauli V Maximi, iussu editum, et a Benedicto XIV, Auctum et Castigatum, Turonibus: Typis a Mame, 1896.

AUTHORS

Aertnys, *Theologia Moralis*, 7 ed., 2 vols., Paderborne, 1906.
Albertus Magnus, *Opera Omnia* in IV Sententias, ex editone Lug-

dunensi Castigata cura ac labore Augusti et Emilii Borguet, 38 vols., Parisiis, 1890-1899.

Aquinas, *Summa Theologica*, 6 vols., Taurine (Italis): Marietti, 1932.

Augustine, *A Commentary on Canon Law*, 8 vols., St. Louis: Herder, 1918-1922.

Ayrinhac-Lydon, *Penal Legislation in the New Code of Canon Law*, New York: Benziger Brothers, 1936.

Ballerini-Palmieri, *Opus Theologicum Morale*, 7 vols., Prati, 1889-1893.

Battifol, *Etudes d'Histoire et de Théologie Positive*, première série, quatrième édition Paris: Librairie Victor Lecoffre, 1906.

Benedict XIV, *De Sacrosancto Missae Sacrificio*, editum a P. Josephus Schneider, Morguntiae: Sumptibus Francisci Kirchheim, 1879.

........, *De Synodo Dioecesana*, 4 vols., Mechliniae, 1842.

Billuart, *Summa Sancti Thomae*, editio nova, 9 vols., Paris: Sumptibus Latouzey et Ane, (no date).

Bingham, *The Antiquities of the Christian Church*, 2 vols., reprinted from the original edition (1708-1722), London, 1878.

Blat, *Commentarium Codicis*, 6 vols., Romae, 1921-1924.

Bona, *Rerum Liturgicarum Libro Duo*, Coloniae, 1674.

Bouscaren, *The Canon Law Digest*, 2 vols. and Supplement, Milwaukee: Bruce, 1936-1937; Supp., 1938.

Brilliant, *Eucharistia*, Encyclopédie Populaire sur l'Eucharistic, Paris: Bloud et Gay, 1934.

Bucceroni, *Theologia Moralis*, 3 ed., 2 vols., Romae, 1898.

Cabrol, *Les Origines Liturgiques*, Paris, 1906.

Capellmann, *Medicina Pastoralis*, 7 ed., Aquisgrani, 1890.

Cappello, *Tractatus Canonico-Moralis de Sacramentis*, Vol. I, *De Sacramentis in Genere, de Baptismo, Confirmatione et Eucharistia*, 3 ed., Romae: Marietti, 1938.

........, *De Censuris*, 3 ed., Romae: Marietti, 1933.

Chardon, *Histoire des Sacrements*, 4 vols., Vol. II, *De l'Eucharistie et de la Pénitence*, Paris, 1745.

Chelodi, *Ius de Personis*, editio altera a Bertagnolli aucta, Trento: Libreria Moderna di a A. Ardesi, 1926.

Cicognani, *Canon Law*, 2 ed., Philadelphia: The Dolphin Press, 1935.

Cocchi, *Commentarium in Codicem Iuris Canonici*, Vol. I, *Normae Generales*, 5 ed., Torino: Marietti, 1938.

Cincina, *Theologia Christiana*, 10 vols., Romae 1749-1751.

Corblet, *Histoire du Sacrement de l'Eucharistie*, 2 vols., Paris, 1885.

Coronata, *Compendium Iuris Canonici*, 2 vols., Taurini: Marietti, 1937-1938.

D'Annibale, *Summula Theologiae Moralis*, 5 ed., 3 vols., Romae, 1908.

Davis, *Moral and Pastoral Theology*, 4 vols., New York: Sheed and Ward Inc., 1935.

De Meester, *Compendium Iuris Canonici*, ed. nova, 3 vols. in 4, Brugis, 1921-1928.

Denzinger-Banwart-Umberg, *Enchiridion Symbolorum Definitionem et Declarationem et Rebus Fidei et Morum*, 21-23 ed., Friburgi Brisgoviae: Herder, 1937.

De Lugo, *Opera Omnia*, edition nova, 8 vols., Vol IV, *De Sacramento Eucharistiae*, Parisiis, 1853.

Devoti, *Institutionem Canonicarum Libri IV*, 2 vols., Leodii, 1860.

Eichman, *Lehrbuch des Kirchenrechts*, 2 ed., Paderborn: Druch and Verlag von Ferdinand Schoningh, 1926.

Elbel-Bierbaum, *Theologia Moralis*, 3 vols., Paderbornae, 1892.
Fortescue, *The Mass, A Study of the Roman Liturgy*, New York, 1912.
Funk, *Manual of Church History*, translated from the fifth German edition by Luigi Cappadelta, St. Louis, 1910.
Gasparri, *Tractatus Canonicus de Sanctissima Eucharistia*, 2 vols., Lugduni, 1897.
Génicot, *Casus Conscientiae*, 2 ed., 2 vols., Lovanii, 1902.
........, *Theologia Moralis*, 2 vols., Lovanii, 1897.
Gennari, *Consultations de Moral de Droit Canonique et de Liturgie*, 5 vols., Paris, 1907-1910.
Goosens, *Les Origines de l'Eucharistie, Sacrement et Sacrifice*, Universitas Catholica Lovaniensis, série II, Tomus 22, Paris: Beauchesne, 1931.
Gury-Ballerini, *Compendium Theologiae Moralis*, 9 ed., 2 vols., Romae, 1889.
Hedley, *The Holy Eucharist*, New York, 1907.
Hefele, *History of the Church Councils*, translated from the German and edited by William Clark, 2 ed., 5 vols., Edinburg, 1883-1896.
........, *Opera Patrum Apostolicorum*, Tubingen, 1874?.
Hefele-Leclercq, *Histoire des Conciles*, 9 vols. in full and Vol. X, Pars I (the set is to run to 12 vols.), Paris, 1909-
Husslein, *The Mass of the Apostles*, New York: Kenedy, 1929.
Jorio, *La Comunione Agl' Infermi*, Roma: Pontificia Libreria Editrice F. Pustet, 1931.
Keating, *The Agape and the Eucharist in the Early Church*, London, 1901.
La Bauche, *The Three Sacraments of Initiation, Baptism, Confirmation, and the Holy Eucharist*, New York: Benziger, 1922.
La Croix, *Theologia Moralis*, 2 vols., Coloniae, 1719.
Lamy, *Dissertatio de Syrorum Fide et Disciplina in Re Eucharistica*, Universitatis Catholica Lovaniensis, Lovanii, 1922.
Landon, *A Manual of Councils of the Holy Catholic Church*, London, 1846.
Layman, *Theologia Moralis, Libri Quinque, Patavii*, 1719.
Lépicier, *Tractatus de Sanctissima Eucharistia*, Pars I, *Tractatus de Sanctissima Eucharistia ut est Sacramentum*, Parisiis: Lethielleux, 1915.
Many, *Praelectiones de Missa cum Appendice de Sanctissimo Sacramento Eucharistiae*, Parisiis, 1903.
Martène, *De Antiquis Ritibus Ecclesiae Libri Tres*, ed. novissima, 3 vols., Rotomagi, 1700-1702.
Merkelbach, *Summa Theologiae Moralis*, 3 vols., Parisiis: Desclee, 1931-1933.
Michiels, *Normae Generales Iuris Canonici*, 2 vols., Lublin, 1929.
Migne, *Patrologiae Cursus Completus, Series Graeca*, 161 vols., Parisiis, 1856-1866.
........, *Patrologiae Cursus Completus, Series Latina*, 221 vols., Parisiis, 1864.
Maroto, *Institutiones Iuris Canonici*, 3 ed., Romae: apud "Commentarium pro Religiosis", (no date).
Noldin, *Summa Theologia Moralis*, 7 ed., 3 vols., Oeniponte, 1908, Vol. III, *De Sacramentis*.
Oietti, *Commentarium in Codicem Canonici*, 4 vols., Romae: apud Aedes Universitatis Gregorianae, 1927-1931.

Pasqualigus, *De Ieiunio, Praxis Ieiunii Ecclesiastici et Naturalis*, Genuae, 1655.

Prat, *La Théologie de St. Paul*, 5ieme édition, Paris, 1913.

Prümmer, *Manuale Theologiae Moralis*, 8 ed., 3 vols., Vol. III, *De Sacramentis in Genere et in Specie*, Friburgi Brisburgiae: Herder, 1936.

Ramsay, *The Church in the Roman Empire*, New York, 1893.

Roberts-Donovan, *Anti-Nicene Fathers*, 10 vols., Translations of the Fathers down to A. D. 325, New York: Scribners, 1903.

Salmanticenses, *Curcus Theologiae Moralis*, 6 vols., Venetiis, 1728.

Sanchez, Thomas, *De Sancto Matrimonii Sacramento*, 3 vols., Lugduni, 1739.

Schaff, *History of the Christian Church*, 7 vols., New York, 1894-1896.

Schroeder, *Disciplinary Decrees of the General Councils, Text, Translation, and Commentary*, St. Louis: Herder, 1937.

Semeria-Berry, *The Eucharistic Liturgy in the Roman Rite*, adapted from the Italian, New York, 1911.

Soto, *Commentarius in Quantum (quem vocant) Sententiarum*, 2 vols., Venetiis, 1575.

Sporer, *Theologia, Moralis Sacramentalis in IV Partes Divisa* 3 ed., Salisburgi, 1711.

Suarez, *Opera Omnia*, editio nova, 30 vols., Vol. XXVII, *De Sacramento Eucharistiae*, Parisiis, 1866.

Tamburini, *Moralis Explicatio Iuris Divini Naturalis et Ecclesiastici*, 1748.

Toso, *Commentaria Minora ad Codicem Iuris Canonici*, Citta de Castello, 1921.

Tummulo-Jorio, *Compendium Theologiae Moralis*, 5 ed., 2 vols., Neapoli, 1935.

Van Hove, Vol. I, *De Consuetudine, de Temporis Supputatione*, Romae: Dessain, 1933.

Vasquez, *Libri Commentariorum ac Disputationum in Tertiam Partem S. Thomae*, 8 vols., Lugduni: Sumptibus, Jacobi Cardon, 1631.

Vermeersch, *Theologia Moralis*, 3 ed., 4 vols., Roma: Università Gregoriana, 1933.

Vermeersch-Creusen, *Epitome Iuris Canonici*, 3 vols., (Vol. I, 6 ed., Vols. II and III, 5 ed.), Romae: Dessain, 1934-1937.

Wernz, *Ius Decretalium*, 6 vols., Romae, 1905-1913.

Woywod, *A Practical Commentary on the Code of Canon Law*, 4 revised edition, 2 vols., New York: Wagner, 1932.

Young, *The Elements of Astronomy*, Boston, 1892.

ARTICLES

Battifol, "Agape,"—*Dictionnaire de Théologie Catholique*, Vacant-Mangenot-Amann, 14 vols., Paris, 1903-1939.

Boudinhon, "A Propos des Aumôniers Militaires et Prêtres Soldats," *Le Canoniste Contemporain* XXXIX (1916), 31-40.

Browe, "Die Neuchternheit vor der Messe und Kommunion im Mittelalter,"—*Ephemerides Liturgicae*, XLV (1931), 279-287.

Cappello, 'De Facultate Concessa Infirmis ex Canone 858, ¶ 2,"—*Periodica*, XXIV (1935), 18*-33*.

Cappello, "Num Mensis, de Quo in Canone 858, ¶ 2, Sit Moraliter Sumendus, an Potius Mathematice,"—*Periodica*, XXIII (1934), 234*-238*.

"Cas de Conscience,"—*Analecta Iuris Pontificii,* XIII (1874), 598-607.
"Circo l'Uso della Pompa Gastrica in Ordine alla SS. Comunione,"—*Il Monitore Ecclesiastico,* IX (1895), 182-184.
Coucke, "De Ieiunio Eucharistico,"—*Collationes Brugenses,* XXXIV (1934), 380-386.
Creusen, "Minuit Canonique" or "La Loi Pure et Simple,"—*Revue Théologique,* L (1923), 464-474.
"De SS. Communione Puerorum Nuper ad S. Synaxim Admissorum, necnon Infirmorum Morbo Chronico Laborantium et Naturale Ieiunium Servare non Valentium,"—*AAS.* XXXIX (1906), 499-510.
"Eucharistic Fast, The"—*The Clergy Review,* III, (1932), 145-146; XV (1938), 251-253; XV (1938), 168-169.
Ferland, "L'Avance de l'Heure et Certains Préceptes de l'Eglise,"—*Semaine Religieuse de Québec,* XXXV (1923), 280-283, 294-298, 567-570, 600-605, 614-621.
Frochisse, "A Propos des Origines du Jeûne Eucharistique,"—*Revue d'Histoire Ecclésiastique de Louvain,* XXVIII (1932), 594-609.
Funk, "L'Agape,"—*Revue d'Histoire Ecclésiastique de Louvain,* IV (1903), 5-22.
.... "Tertullien et l'Agape,"—*Revue d'Histoire Ecclésiastique* de Louvain, V (1904), 5-15.
Gillis, "The Christian Agape,"—*Catholic University Bulletin,* IX (1903), 465-508.
Harty, "The Natural Fast,"—*IER,* 4 series, XXV (1909), 307-308.
Kinane, "Celebration of Mass by a Priest Excused from Fasting,"—*IER,* 5 series, IX (1917), 226-227.
........, "The Eucharistic Fast—The Decree of 1906; What Class of Persons Are Affected,"—*IER,* 5 series, III (1914), 416-420.
........, "Some Queries in Regard to the Modification of the Eucharistic Fast for the Sick,"—*IER,* XXXV (1930), 519-521.
Ladeuze, "Pas d'Agape dans la Première Epître aux Corinthiens,"—*Revue Biblique,* I (1904), 78-81.
"Les Lavages de l'Estomac et le Sainte Communion,"—*Le Canoniste Contemporain,* XX (1897), 141-144.
MacCarthy, "The Eucharistic Fast,"—*ER,* LXIX (1923), 183-189.
Mahoney, "The Eucharistic Fast,"—*The Clergy Review,* IV (1932), 70-71.
Mitchell, "True Sun Time,"—*ER,* XC (1934), 77-83.
........, "What Time Is It? Midnight and Fasting,"—*ER,* LXXXIV (1931) 491-500.
Murray, "The Fast before Holy Communion,"—*Homiletic Monthly and Pastoral Review,* 2 series, XXV (1925), 976-978.
Nevin, "Duplicating after the Fast Is Broken,"—*Australasian Catholic Record,* I, n. 3 (1924), 35-36.
O'Donnell, "Administration of the Viaticum to Soldiers Ordered to the Front,"—*IER,* 5 series, VI (1915), 625-627.
O'Neil, "A Case Concerning the Eucharistic Fast,"—*IER,* 5 series, XXVI (1925), 401-402.
........, "The Eucharistic Fast,"—*IER,* XXI (1923), 524-528.
Richarz, "Computing Time According to Canon Law,"—*ER,* LXXXVII (1932), 176-180.
Rongy, "L'Abus des Corinthiens dans la Célébration de l'Eucharistie,"—*Revue Ecclésiastique de Liège,* I (1929), 421-434.

Tachy, "Etude Canonique et Liturgie sur le Binage,"—*Revue des Sciences Ecclésiastiques*, XLVII (1883), 510-514.
Thomas, "L'Agape,"—*Dictionnaire de la Bible*, I, Suppl. (1928).
Thurston, "My Sacrifice and Yours,"—*Ecclesiastical Review*, XCI (1934), 565-577.
Twomey, "The Eucharistic Fast,"—*ER*, CII (1940), 416.
Vermeersch, "Dispensatio a Ieiunio Eucharistico ante Missam Celebrationem,"—*Periodica*, XXI (1932), 105-108.
........, "Ieiunium ante Missam,"—*Periodica*, XII (1923), 29-32.
........, "Recta Computatio Mensis, Quo Elapso, Licet Semel vel Bis in Hebdomada, Decumbenti Infirmo Permittere ut S. Dape Reficiatur Postquam Aliquid per Modum Potus vel Medicinae Sumpserit,"—*Periodica*, XXIII (1934), 61*-63*.
Villien, "La Dispense du Jeûne Eucharistique pour les Prêtres,"—*Le Canoniste Contemporain*, XLVI (1924), 1-17.
Woywod, "Daylight Saving Time and the Obligations in Which the Point of Time Is Important,"—*Homiletic Monthly and Pastoral Review*, 2 series, XXXVII (1927), 962-964.

PERIODICALS

American Ecclesiastical Review, Philadelphia, 1889-
Analecta Iuris Pontificii, Romae, 1871—
Australasian Catholic Record, The, Manly, 1923—
Catholic University Bulletin, Washington, D. C., 1895—
Clergy Review, The, London, 1931—
Collationes Brugenses, Brugis Flandorum, 1895.
Ecclesiastical Review, The (formerly the American Ecclesiastical Review), Philadelphia, 1889—
Ephemerides Liturgicae, Commentarium cura et studio Presbyterorum Congregationis Missionis Nonnullis Doctis Variis Adlaborantibus Alterius Mensibus Editum, Roma: Via Pompeo Magno, 21, 1886—
Homiletic Monthly and Pastoral Review, New York, 1900—
Irish Ecclesiastical Record, Dublin, 1864—
Ius Pontificium, Romae, 1921—
L'Ami du Clergé, Paris, 1879—
Le Canoniste Contemporain, Paris, 1878—
Monitore Ecclesiastico, Il, Romae, 1876—
Nouvelle Revue Théologique, Parisiis, 1869—
Periodica de Re Canonica et Morali utili praesertim Religiosis et Missionariis, Brugis, 1905—; ab anno 1927: *Periodica de Re Morali, Canonica, Liturgica.*
Revue des Sciences Ecclésiastiques, Paris, 1860—
Revue Théologique, Paris, 1856—
Theologisch-praktische Quartalschrift, Linz, 1832—

ABBREVIATIONS

AAS—Acta Apostolicae Sedis.
ASS—Acta Sanctae Sedis.
Coll. S. C. P. F.—Collectanea of the Sacred Congregation of the Propagation of the Faith.
ER—The Ecclesiastical Review.
Fontes—Codicis Iuris Canonici Fontes.
IER—Irish Ecclesiastical Record.
Mansi—Sacrorum Conciliorum Nova et Amplissima Collectio.
MPG—Migne, Patrologia, Series Graeca.

MPL—Migne, Patrologia, Series Latina.
PCI—The Pontifical Commission for the Authentic Interpretation of the Code.
Periodica—Periodica de Re Morali, Canonica, Liturgica.
S. C. C.—Sacred Congregation of the Councils.
S. C. R.—Sacred Congregation of Rites.
S. C. Sacr.—Sacred, Congregation of the Sacraments.
S. C. S. Off.—Sacred Congregation of the Holy Office.

BIOGRAPHICAL NOTE

Thomas F. Anglin was born on August 5, 1912, in New Haven, Connecticut. He attended St. Francis parochial school of that city for his elementary education, and the preparatory seminary of the Missionaries of Our Lady of LaSalette in Hartford, Conn. After his novitiate he entered LaSalette Seminary in Altamont, N.Y., where he made his philosophical and theological studies. He was ordained to the priesthood on June 11, 1938. That same year he went to Rome where he attended the Gregorian University, from which he received his Baccalaureate in Canon Law in June, 1939. Upon his return from Rome he entered the School of Canon Law of the Catholic University of America to complete his studies, and there received the degree of the Licentiate in Canon Law in June, 1940.

INDEX

CANON LAW STUDIES

1. Freriks, Rev. Celestine A., C.PP.S., J.C.D., Religious Congregations in Their External Relations, 121 pp., 1916.
2. Galliher, Rev. Daniel M., O.P., J.C.D., Canonical Elections, 117 pp., 1917.
3. Borkowski, Rev. Aurelius L., O.F.M., J.C.D., De Confraternitatibus Ecclesiasticis, 136 pp., 1918.
4. Castillo, Rev. Cayo, J.C.D., Disertracion Historico-Canonica sobre la Potestad del Cabildo en Sede Vacante o Impedida del Vicario Capitular, 99 pp., 1919 (1918).
5. Kubelbeck, Rev. William J., S.T.B., J.C.D., The Sacred Pentitentiaria and Its Relations to Faculties of Ordinaries and Priests, 129 pp., 1918.
6. Petrovits, Rev. Joseph J.C., S.T.D., J.C.D., The New Church Law On Matrimony, X-461 pp., 1919.
7. Hickey, Rev. John J., S.T.B., J.C.D., Irregularities and Simple Impediments in the New Code of Canon Law, 100 pp., 1920.
8. Klekotka, Rev. Peter J., S.T.B., J.C.D., Diocesan Consultors, 179 pp., 1920.
9. Wanenmacher, Rev. Francis, J.C.D., The Evidence in Ecclesiastical Procedure Affecting the Marriage Bond, 1920 (Printed 1935).
10. Golden, Rev. Henry Francis, J.C.D., Parochial Benefices in the New Code, IV,119 pp., 1921 (Printed 1925).
11. Koudelka, Rev. Charles J., J.C.D., Pastors, Their Rights and Duties According to the New Code of Canon Law, 211 pp., 1921.
12. Melo, Rev. Antonius, O.F.M., J.C.D., De Exemptione Regularium, X-188 pp., 1921.
13. Schaaf, Rev. Valentine Theodore, O.F.M., S.T.B., J.C.D., The Cloister, X-180 pp., 1921.
14. Burke, Rev. Thomas Joseph, S.T.D., J.C.D., Competence in Ecclesiastical Tribunals, IV-117 pp., 1922.
15. Leech, Rev. George Leo, J.C.D., A Comparative Study of the Constitution, "Apostolicae Sedis" and the "Codex Juris Canonici," 179 pp., 1922.
16. Motry, Rev. Hubert Louis, S.T.D., J.C.D., Diocesan Faculties According to the Code of Canon Law, II-167 pp., 1922.
17. Murphy, Rev. George Lawrence, J.C.D., Delinquencies and Penalties in the Administration and Reception of the Sacraments, IV-121 pp., 1923.

18. O'Reilly, Rev. John Anthony, S.T.B., J.C.D., Ecclesiastical Sepulture in the New Code of Canon Law, II-129 pp., 1923.
19. Michalicka, Rev. Wencelas Cyrill, O.S.B., J.S.D., Judicial Procedure in Dismissal of Clerical Exempt Religious, 107 pp., 1923.
20. Dargin, Rev. Edward Vincent, S.T.B., J.C.D., Reserved Cases According to the Code of Canon Law, IV-103 pp., 1924.
21. Godfrey, Rev. John A., S.T.B., J.C.D., The Right of Patronage According to the Code of Canon Law, 153 pp., 1924.
22. Hagedorn, Rev. Francis Edward, J.C.D., General Legislation on Indulgences, II-154 pp., 1924.
23. King, Rev. James Ignatius, J.C.D., The Administration of the Sacraments to Dying Non-Catholics, V-141 pp., 1924.
24. Winslow, Rev. Francis Joseph, A.F.M., J.C.D., Vicars and Prefects Apostolic, IV-149 pp., 1924.
25. Correa, Rev. Jose Servelion, S.T.L., J.C.D., La Potestad Legislativa de la Iglesia Catolica, IV-127 pp., 1925.
26. Dugan, Rev. Henry Francis, A.M., J.C.D., The Judiciary Department of the Diocesan Curia, 87 pp., 1925.
27. Keller, Rev. Charles Frederick, S.T.B., J.C.D., Mass Stipends, 167 pp., 1925.
28. Paschang, Rev. John Linus, J.C.D., The Sacramentals According to the Code of Canon Law, 129 pp., 1925.
29. Pointek, Rev. Cyrillus, O.F.M., S.T.B., J.C.D., De Indulto Exclaustrationis necnon Saecularizationis, XIII-289 pp., 1925.
30. Kearney, Rev. Richard Joseph, S.T.B., J.C.D., Sponsor at Baptism According to the Code of Canon Law, IV-127 pp., 1925.
31. Bartlett, Rev. Chester Joseph, A.M., LL.B., J.C.D., The tenure of Parochial Property in the United States of America, V-108 pp., 1926.
32. Kilker, Rev. Adrian Jerome, J.C.D., Extreme Unction, V-425 pp., 1926.
33. McCormick, Rev. Robert Emmett, J.C.D., Confessors of Religious, VII-266 pp., 1926.
34. Miller, Rev. Newton Thomas, J.S.D., Founded Masses According to the Code of Canon Law, VII-93 pp., 1926.
35. Roelker, Rev. Edward G., S.T.D., J.C.D., Principles of Privilege According to the Code of Canon Law, XI-166 pp., 1926.
36. Bakalarczyk, Rev. Richardus, M.I.C., J.U.D., De Novitiatu, VIII-208 pp., 1927.
37 Pizzuti, Rev. Lawrence, O.F.M., J.U.L., De Parochis Religiosis, 1927. (Not printed).
38. Bliley, Rev. Nicholas Martin, O.S.B., J.C.D., Altars According to the Code of Canon Law, XIX-132 pp., 1927.
39. Brown, Mr. Brendan Francis, A.B., LL.M., J.U.D., The Canoni-

cal Juristic Personality with Special Reference to Its Status in the United States of America, V-212 pp., 1927.

40. Cavanaugh, Rev. William Thomas, C.P., J.U.D., The Reservation of the Blessed Sacrament, VIII-101 pp., 1927.
41. Doheny, Rev. William J., C.S.C., A.B., J.U.D., Church Property: Modes of Acquisition, X-118 pp., 1927.
42. Feldhaus, Rev. Aloysius H., C.PP.S., J.C.D., Oratories, IX-141 pp., 1927.
43. Kelly, Rev. James Patrick, A.B., J.C.D., The Jurisdiction of the Simple Confessor, X-208 pp., 1927.
44. Neuberger, Rev. Nicholas J., J.C.D., Canon 6 or the Relation of the Codex Juris Canonici to the Preceding Legislation, V-95 pp., 1927.
45. O'Keefe, Rev. Gerald Michael, J.C.D., Matrimonial Dispensations, Powers of Bishops, Priests and Confessors, VIII-232 pp., 1927.
46. Quigley, Rev. Joseph A.M., A.B., J.C.B., Condemned Societies, 139 pp., 1927.
47. Zaplotnik, Rev. Johannes Leo, J.C.D., De Vicariis Foraneis, X-142 pp., 1927.
48. Duskie, Rev. John Alyosius, A.B., J.C.D., The Canonical Status of the Orientals in the United States, VIII-196 pp., 1928.
49. Hyland, Rev. Francis Edward, J.C.D., Excommunication, Its Nature, Historical Development and Effects, VIII-181 pp., 1928.
50. Reinmann, Rev. Gerald Joseph, O.M.C., J.C.D., The Third Order Secular of Saint Francis, 201 pp., 1928.
51. Schenk, Francis J., J.C.D., The Matrimonial Impediments of Mixed Religion and Disparity of Cult, XVI-318 pp., 1929.
52. Coady, Rev. John Joseph, S.T.D., J.C.D., A.M., The Appointment of Pastors, VIII-150 pp., 1929.
53. Kay, Rev. Thomas Henry, J.C.D., Competence in Matrimonial Procedure, VIII-164 pp., 1929.
54. Turner, Rev. Sidney Joseph, C.P., J.U.D., The Vow of Poverty, XLIX-217 pp., 1929.
55. Kearney, Rev. Raymond, A., A.B., S.T.D., J.C.D., The Principles, of Delegation, VII-149 pp., 1929.
56. Conran, Rev. Edward James, A.B., J.C.D., The Interdict, V-163 pp., 1930.
57. O'Neil, Rev. William H., J.C.D., Papal Rescripts of Favor, VII-218 pp., 1930.
58. Bastnagel, Rev. Clement Vincent, J.U.D., The Appointment of Parochial Adjutants and Assistants, XV-257 pp., 1930.
59. Ferry, Rev. William A., A.B., J.C.D., Stole Fees, V-135 pp., 1930.
60. Costello, Rev. John Michael, A.B., J.C.D., Domicile and Quasi-domicile, VII-201 pp., 1930.

61. Kremer, Rev. Michael Nicholas, A.B., S.T.B., J.C.D., Church Support in the United States, VI-1930.
62. Angulo, Rev. Luis, C.M., J.C.D., Legislation de la Iglesia sobre la intencion en la application de la Santa Misa, VII-104 pp., 1931.
63. Frey, Rev. Wolfgang Norbert, O.S.B., A.B., J.C.D., The Act of Religious Profession, VII-174 pp., 1931.
64. Roberts, Rev. James Brendan, A.B., J.C.D., The Banns of Marriage, XIV-140 pp., 1931.
65. Ryder, Rev. Raymond Aloysius, A.B., J.C.D., Simony, IX-151 pp., 1931.
66. Campagna, Rev. Angelo, Ph.D., J.U.D., Il Vicario Generale del Vescovo, VII-205 pp., 1931.
67. Cox, Rev. Joseph Godfrey, A.B., J.C.D., The Administration of Seminaries, VI-124 pp., 1931.
68. Gregory, Rev. Donald J., J.U.D., The Pauline Privilege, XV-165 pp., 1931.
69. Donohue, Rev. John F., J.C.D., The Impediment of Crime, VII-110 pp., 1931.
70. Dooley, Rev. Eugene A., O.M.I., J.C.D., Church Law On Sacred Relics, IX-143 pp., 1931.
71. Orth, Rev. Raymond Clement, O.M.C., J.C.D., The Approbation of Religious Institutes, 171 pp., 1931.
72. Pernicone, Rev. Joseph M., A.B., J.C.D., The Ecclesiastical Prohibition of Books, XII-267 pp., 1932.
73. Clinton, Rev. Connell, A.B., J.C.D., The Paschal Precept, IX-108 pp., 1932.
74. Donnelly, Rev. Francis B., A.M., S.T.L., J.C.D., The Diocesan Synod, VII-125 pp., 1932.
75. Torrente, Rev. Camilo, C.M.F., J.C.D., Las Processiones Sagradas, V-145 pp., 1932.
76. Murphy, Rev. Edwin J., C.PP.S., J.C.D., Suspension Ex Informata Conscientia, XI-122 pp., 1932.
77. Mackenzie, Rev. Eric, F., A.M., S.T.L., J.C.D., The Delict of Heresy in its Commission, Penalization, Absolution, VII-124 pp., 1932.
78. Lyons, Rev. Avitus E., S.T.B., J.C.D., The Collegiate Tribunal of First Instance, XI-47 pp., 1932.
79. Connolly, Rev. Thomas A., J.C.D., Appeals, XI-195 pp., 1932.
80. Sangmeister, Rev. Joseph V., A.B., J.C.D., Force and Fear as Precluding Matrimonial Consent, V-211 pp., 1932.
81. Jaeger, Rev. Leo A., A.B., J.C.D., The Administration of Vacant and Quasi-vacant Episcopal Sees in the United States, IX-229 pp., 1932.

82. Rimlinger, Rev. Herbert T., J.C.D., Error Invalidating Matrimonial Consent, VII-79 pp,, 1932.
83. Barret, Rev. John D. M., S.S., J.C.D., A Comparative Study of the Third Plenary Council of Baltimore and the Code, IX-221 pp., 1932.
84. Carberry, Rev. John J. Ph.D., S.T.D., J.C.D., The Juridical Form of Marriage, X-177 pp., 1934.
85. Dolan, Rev. John L., A.B., J.C.D., The Defensor Vinculi, XII-157 pp., 1934.
86. Hannan, Rev. Jerome D., A.M., S.T.D., LL.B., J.C.D., The Canon Law of Wills, IX-517 pp., 1934.
87. Lemieux, Rev. Delisle A., A.M., J.C.D., The Sentence in Ecclesiastical Procedure, IX-131 pp., 1934.
88. O'Rourke, Rev. James J., A.B., J.C.D., Parish Registers, VII-109 pp., 1934.
89. Timlin, Rev. Bartholomew, O.F.M., A.M., J.C.D., Conditional Matrimonial Consent, X-381 pp., 1934.
90. Wahl, Rev. Francis X., A.B., J.C.D., The Matrimonial Impediments of Consanguinity and Affinity, VI-125 pp., 1934.
91. White, Rev. Robert J., A.B., LL.B., S.T.B., J.C.D., Canonical Ante-Nuptial Promises and the Civil Law, VI-152 pp., 1934.
92. Herrera, Rev. Antonio Parra, O.C.D., J.C.D., Legislation Ecclesiastica sobra el Ayuno y la Abstinencia, XI-191 pp., 1935.
93. Kennedy, Rev. Edwin J., J.C.D., The Special Matrimonial Process in Cases of Evidént Nullity, X-165 pp., 1935.
94. Manning, Rev. John J., A.B., J.C.D., Presumption of Law in Matrimonial Procedure, XI-111 pp., 1935.
95. Moeder, Rev. John M., J.C.D., The Proper Bishop for Ordination and Dismissorial Letters, VII-135 pp., 1935.
96. O'Mara, Rev. William A., A.B., J.C.D., Canonical Causes For Matrimonial Dispensations, IX-155 pp., 1935.
97. Reilly, Rev. Peter, J.C.D., Residence of Pastors, IX-81 pp., 1935.
98. Smith, Rev. Mariner T., O.P., S.T.L., J.C.D., The Penal Law For Religious, VII-169 pp., 1935.
99. Whalen, Rev. Donald W., A.M., J.C.D., The Value of Testimonial Evidence in Matrimonial Procedure, XIII-297 pp., 1935.
100. Cleary, Rev. Joseph F., J.C.D., Canonical Limitations on the Alienation of Church Property, VIII-141 pp., 1936.
101. Glynn, Rev. John C., J.C.D., The Promoter of Justice, XX-337 pp., 1936.
102. Brennan, Rev. James H., S.S., A.M., S.T.B., J.C.D., The Simple Convalidation of Marriage, VI-135 pp., 1937.
103. Brunini, Rev. Joseph Bernard, J.C.D., The Clerical Obligations of Canons, 139 and 142, X-121 pp., 1937.

104. Connor, Rev. Maurice, A.B., J.C.D., The Administrative Removal of Pastors, VIII-159 pp., 1937.
105. Guilfoyle, Rev. Merlin Joseph, J.C.D., Custom, XI-144 pp., 1937.
106. Hughes, Rev. James Austin, A.B., A.M., J.C.D., Witnesses in Criminal Trials of Clerics, IX-140 pp., 1937.
107. Jansen, Rev. Raymond J., A.B., S.T.L., J.C.D., Canonical Provisions for Catechetical Instruction, VII-153 pp., 1937.
108. Kealy, Rev. John James, A.B., J.C.D., The Introductory Libellus in Church Court Procedure, XI-121 pp., 1937.
109. McManus, Rev. James Edward, C.SS.R., J.C.D., The Administration of Temporal Goods in Religious Institutes, XVI-196 pp., 1937.
110. Moriarity, Rev. Eugene James, J.C.D., Oaths in Ecclesiastical Courts, X-115 pp., 1937.
111. Rainer, Rev. Eligius George, C.SS.R., J.C.D., Suspension of Clerics, XVII-249 pp., 1937.
112. Reilly, Rev. Thomas F., C.SS.R., J.C.D., Visitation of Religious, VI-195 pp., 1938.
113. Moriarty, Rev. Francis E., C.SS.R., J.C.D., The Extraordinary Absolution from Censures, XV-334 pp., 1938.
114. Connolly, Rev. Nicholas P., J.C.D., The Canonical Erection of Parishes, X-132 pp., 1938.
115. Donovan, Rev. James Joseph, J.C.D., The Pastor's Obligation in Prenuptial Investigation, XII-322 pp., 1938.
116. Harrigan, Rev. Robert J., M.A., S.T.B., J.C.D., The Radical Sanation of Invalid Marriages, VII-208 pp., 1938.
117. Boffa, Rev. Conrad Humbert, J.C.D., Canonical Provisions for Catholic Schools, X-211 pp., 1939.
118. Parsons, Rev. Anscar John, O.M. Cap., J.C.D., Canonical Elections, XII-236 pp., 1939.
119. Reilly, Rev. Edward Michael, A.B., J.C.D., The General Norms of Dispensation, X-156 pp., 1939.
120. Ryan, Rev. Gerald Aloysius, A.B., J.C.D., Principles of Episcopal Jurisdiction, XII-172 pp., 1939.
121. Burton, Rev. Francis James, C.S.C., A.B., J.C.D., A Commentary on Canon 1125, X-222 pp., 1940.
122. Miaskiewicz, Rev. Francis Sigismund, J.C.D., Supplied Jurisdiction according to Canon 209, XII-340 pp., 1940.
123. Rice, Rev. Patrick William, A.B., J.C.D., Proof of Death in Prenuptial Investigation, VIII-156 pp., 1940.
124. Anglin, Rev. Thomas Francis, M.S., J.C.L., The Eucharistic Fast.
125. Colman, Rev. John Jerome, J.C.L., The Minister of Confirmation.
126. Downs, Rev. John Emmanuel, A.B., J.C.L., The Concept of Clerical Immunity.

127. Esswein, Rev. Anthony Albert, J.C.L., Extrajudicial Penal Powers of Ecclesiastical Superiors.
128. Farrell, Rev. Benjamin Francis, M.A., S.T.L., J.C.L., The Rights and Duties of the Local Ordinary Regarding Congregations of Women Religious of Pontificial Approval.
129. Feeney, Rev. Thomas John, A.B., S.T.L., J.C.L., Restitutio in Integrum.
130. Findlay, Rev. Stephen William, O.S.B., A.B., J.C.L., Canonical Norms Governing the Deposition and Degradation of Clerics.
131. Goodwine, Rev. John, A.B., S.T.L., J.C.L., The Right of the Church to Acquire Property.
132. Heston, Rev. Edward Louis, C.S.C., Ph.D., S.T.D., J.C.L., The Alienation of Church Property in the United States.
133. Hogan, Rev. James John, S.T.L., J.C.L., Judicial Advocates and Procurators.
134. Kealy, Rev. Thomas M., A.B., Litt. B., J.C.L., Dowry of Women Religious.
135. Keene, Rev. Michael James, O.S.B., J.C.L., Religious Ordinaries and Canon 198.
136. Kerin, Rev. Charles A., S.S., M.A., S.T.B., J.C.L., The Privation of Christian Burial.
137. Louis, Rev. William Francis, M.A., J.C.L., Diocesan Archives.
138. McDevitt, Rev. Gilbert Joseph, A.B., J.C.L., Legitimacy and Legitimation.
139. McDonough, Rev. Thomas Joseph, A.B., J.C.L., Apostolic Administrators.
140. Meier, Rev. Carl Anthony, A.B., J.C.L., Penal Administrative Procedure Against Negligent Pastors.
141. Schmidt, Rev. John Rogg, A.B., J.C.L., The Principles of Authentic Interpretation in Canon 17 of the Code of Canon Law.
142. Slafkowsky, Rev. Andrew Leonard, A.B., J.C.L., The Canonical Episcopal Visitation of the Diocese.
143. Swoboda, Rev. Innocent Robert, O.F.M., J.C.L., Ignorance in Relation to the Imputability of Delicts.
144. Dubé, Rev. Arthur Joseph, A.B., J.C.L., The General Principles for the Reckoning of Time in Canon Law.
145. McBride, Rev. James T., A.B., J.C.L., Incardination and Excardination of Seculars.